When Grief is Complicated

Edited by Kenneth J. Doka and Amy S. Tucci

HOSPICE FOUNDATION
OF AMERICA

This book is part of Hospice Foundation of America's *Living with Grief* series.

Ordering information:

Call Hospice Foundation of America: 800-854-3402

Or write:
Hospice Foundation of America
1707 L Street, NW Suite 220
Washington, DC 20036

Or visit HFA's online:
www.hospicefoundation.org

Managing Editor: Lisa McGahey Veglahn
Layout and Design: HBP, Inc.

Publisher's Cataloging-in-Publication
(Provided by Quality Books, Inc.)

   When grief is complicated / edited by Kenneth J. Doka and
   Amy S. Tucci.
      pages cm. – (Living with grief series)
      Includes bibliographical references and index.
      LCCN 2016953396
      ISBN 9781893349216

   1. Grief. 2. Grief therapy. I. Doka, Kenneth J.,
editor. II. Tucci, Amy S., editor. III. Series: Living
with grief.

BF575.G7W475 2017   155.9'37
                            QBI16-900048

Dedication

To Pawnee and Carson Rowe

*Caring brothers whose inner strength
and resilience serves them well
as they journey through life*

KJD

*To William Creedon, Sarah Kelly, Jayne Liu,
Timothy Pellegrino, and Irene Putzig*

*Thank you for your energy, hard work, and service
to Hospice Foundation of America and its constituents*

We will not forget you

AST

Contents

Acknowledgments

Wе always begin by thanking our small staff of the Hospice Foundation of America, especially Lindsey Currin, Cindy Bramble, and Kristen Nanjundaram. It is incredible how, year after year, we produce webinars, *Journeys: A Newsletter to Help in Bereavement,* as well as our *Living with Grief*® program and book, with such a small staff.

We also thank a supportive Board of Directors for all their ongoing efforts. Their counsel keeps us grounded and the Foundation running.

Special recognition goes to our managing editor, Lisa McGahey Veglahn, who keeps us on deadline and carefully reviews all aspects of production. Lisa is more than a managing editor; she acts as our first critic, catching every error and clarifying every assumption.

Naturally we also need to thank the authors who responded to tight deadlines, numerous queries, requests for revisions, and the travails that editors inevitably bring. We so much appreciate how they bring their theoretical expertise and clinical skills to each chapter.

Both editors would like to thank their families and friends for their patience as we worked to publish a book in such a short time. They are commended for their understanding and support as we all seem to go into a state of editorial hibernation (or rather, hyperactivity).

The Hospice Foundation of America exists and produces so much with the assistance of our partners, sponsors, and many contributors. We are grateful for all their help.

As always, we wish to recognize the continuing legacy of the late Jack Gordon, former chair of the Hospice Foundation of America, and David Abrams, former president, current board member, and always friend.

The Nature of Complicated Grief

The late Phyllis Silverman, a pioneer in the study of grief, used to say that "grief is not complicated, people are complicated." Yet the reality is that complex people, convoluted relationships, and complicated and traumatic deaths can engender complicated grief. Freud (1917) recognized that a century ago. In his paper, *Mourning and Melancholia,* Freud attempted to differentiate the normal experience of grief from one of its abnormal variants, depression.

Yet, the debate continues. One of the reasons that Hospice Foundation of America selected the topic "When Grief is Complicated" for exploration is that this debate intensified prior to the newest revision of the American Psychiatric Association's *Diagnostic and Statistical Manual of Mental Disorders* (5th ed.; *DSM-5;* 2013). The *DSM* had previously not recognized any form of complicated grief. As Doka notes in the opening chapter, as the work of revision on the *DSM* began, several diagnoses were suggested. The most prominent were prolonged grief disorder and complicated grief, as well as suggested revisions to other disorders such as major depressive disorder. While some of these suggestions were acted upon, others were deferred, and a few generated considerable controversy.

One of the concerns expressed during the revision process was that if the authors did name a specific syndrome for complicated grief, there would also be recognition included that there may be many ways complications to grief are manifested (see Rando et al., 2012). Worden, in his chapter, notes his earlier work in which he identified four such syndromes. Chronic grief refers to grief that seems to be unusually long in duration. Rather than the normal amelioration that grievers generally experience, grief does not seem to abate in the chronic form. In exaggerated grief, certain symptoms, such as anger or guilt, may seem intense and out of proportion. Worden also identifies delayed grief. Here the griever may experience what seems to be a relatively minimal reaction at the time of loss, only to have a much more intense reaction at some later time, triggered by a subsequent loss or reaching a milestone event. Finally, Worden acknowledges masked grief, where another problem, such as alcohol or substance abuse, anorexia, or acting out behaviors, is the identified problem, but underlying those problems is the issue of grief.

The key to identifying complicated grief is that it significantly impairs the grieving individual's ability to function in key roles, whether at home, work, or in school. Webb uses the concept of disabling grief to describe when grief interferes with the basic ability to function. Webb's chapter is valuable in a number of ways. The case studies clearly illustrate, through examples with children, adolescents, and adults, the varied ways that grief can impair the ability to function. Webb provides both a careful analysis of each case and the therapeutic approach she used in these cases.

The two final chapters of this section offer caveats. Rosenblatt reminds that grief is a cultural construct; in different cultures or subcultures, what are considered normal responses to loss can vary considerably. This is a sage reminder to therapists to always consider the cultural context and grieving norms in assessing complicated grief. It is a point well-recognized and reaffirmed by Stroebe and her associates in their book on complicated grief. They define complicated grief "as a clinically significant deviation from the cultural norm in either (a) the time course or intensity of specific or general symptoms of grief and/ or (b) the level of impairment in social, occupational or other areas of functioning" (Stroebe, Hansson, Schut, & Stroebe, 2008, p. 7).

In addition to the admonition, other themes run through Rosenblatt's chapter. Therapists have to acknowledge the ways that cultural constraints and social issues such as perceived injustice can complicate grief.

Finally, Schuurman's chapter closes many circles. She reaffirms Silverman's comment that people, rather than grief, can be complicated, and strongly cautions against pathologizing what is, for many people, a normal response to a heart-breaking loss. She worries that such a tendency may lead to bereaved individuals being medicated rather than socially or therapeutically supported. Schuurman echoes Rosenblatt's point about the ways that social factors may influence the definition and course of complicated grief. Schuurman stresses how the interests of the therapeutic community and the pharmaceutical industries have a stake in pathologizing grief. Yet, in the end, each chapter reaffirms a central point: while grief is a normal transitional event in the lives of most people, some individuals do have complications in coping with loss that merit support and treatment.

REFERENCES

Freud, S. (1917). Mourning and melancholia. In Strachey, J. (Ed. and Trans., 1961). *The standard edition of the complete psychological works of Sigmund Freud,* Vol. 14: 243-258. London, UK: Hogarth Press.

Rando, T. A., Doka, K. J., Fleming, S., Franco, M. H., Lobb, E., Parkes, C. M., & Steele, R. (2012). A call to the field: Complicated grief in the *DSM-5. OMEGA—Journal of Death and Dying, 65*(4), 263-267.

Stroebe, M., Hansson, R., Schut, H., & Stroebe, W. (2008). *Handbook of bereavement research and practice.* Washington, DC: American Psychological Association.

CHAPTER 1

Complicated Grief in the *DSM-5*: A Brief Review

Kenneth J. Doka

Since the earliest scientific study of grief, there has been recognition that for most individuals, grief following a death is a normal, albeit difficult, transition, but that some individuals will have a more complicated reaction to such loss. These complications can be manifested in physical and psychological health and well-being. Though loss is an event that most people will encounter multiple times during their lives, loss does not get easier with practice. Each event can be a severely stressful experience.

Yet, despite the wide recognition of the potentially deleterious complications of grief, it received little attention in past editions of the *Diagnostic and Statistical Manual of Mental Disorders (DSM)*, the authoritative manual of the American Psychiatric Association (APA) that classifies varied forms of mental disorders. The prior edition of the *DSM*, the *DSM IV-TR*, only listed bereavement under "other conditions that might be the focus of clinical attention," a sort of catch-all category that included a variety of conditions other than mental disorders such as sexual dysfunctions, marital difficulties, occupational difficulties, social problems, or educational difficulties that might cause an individual to seek counseling. This distinction is important, as the *DSM* not only validates a diagnosis but also establishes a requirement for insurance reimbursement through its diagnostic codes (APA, 2000).

More recently, as the APA was developing the newest edition of the *DSM*, the *DSM-5*, there were initiatives, some highly debated and controversial, to recognize more complicated variants of grief (2013). This chapter explores those arguments, indicating the ways that complicated grief is acknowledged in the *DSM-5* as well as some of the areas where a consensus was not reached. The chapter will first define complicated grief as well as briefly review some of the earlier approaches to understanding and classifying complicated grief.

DEFINING COMPLICATED GRIEF: A REVIEW

Over the years, complicated grief has been defined in a number of ways. Rando, for example, defines complicated grief as "a generic term indicating that, given the amount of time since the death, there is some compromise, distortion, or failure of one or more of the processes of mourning" (1993, p.12). Stroebe, Hansson, Schut, and Stroebe defined it as a "clinically significant deviation from the cultural norm in either (a) the time or intensity of specific or general symptoms of grief and/or (b) the level of impairment in social, occupational, or other important areas of functioning" (2008, p. 7). These definitions add three critical elements to a definition of complicated grief. First, they emphasize that something has occurred that has distorted acute or typical grief in some way. Second, the definitions recognize that complicated grief should always be understood within the cultural context in which it occurs. What seems like a distortion in one culture (e.g., hysterical crying or throwing oneself into an open grave) may be perceived as excessive emotionality, while in another culture it may be normative. Finally, these conceptualizations of complicated grief acknowledge that the grief significantly, and over time, effectively impairs a bereaved individual's ability to function in key occupational, familial, social, or educational roles.

Complicated grief was acknowledged in the very beginnings of the scientific study of grief. Freud's 1917 paper, *Mourning and Melancholia*, is often viewed as one of the earliest and defining contributions to the study of grief. Here Freud attempted to differentiate the normal process of mourning from the more complicated variant of melancholia, or what today is characterized as a major depressive disorder. A few years earlier, Shand (1914) noted four types of grief responses, indicating that some might involve depressive, manic, or suppressive reactions.

In 1937, Deutsch introduced the notion of absent grief as another anomaly or atypical pattern. While Freud emphasized that grief can be complicated when it is too intense or lasts too long, Deutsch (1937) added that unexpressed grief is also problematic and often results when there is an absence of social support. In some ways, Deutsch foreshadows subsequent work on disenfranchised grief (Doka, 1989, 2002) as a factor that can complicate the mourning process. Many years later, Worden (2009) would draw on Deutsch's work in his discussion of both delayed and masked grief. Deutsch's brief paper presaged much of the later work on complicated grief as she affirmed that "the work of mourning does not always follow a normal course. It may be excessively intense, even violent, or that the process may be unduly prolonged to the point of chronicity" (1937, p. 12).

In one of the first empirical studies of grief, Lindemann (1944) described grief as a syndrome with clear physical and psychological symptomatology. Lindemann also recognized, in this influential work, that while normal grief follows a predictable course, it can become distorted and lead to more complicated variants.

Both Rando (1993) and Worden (2009) listed a series of distinct syndromes of complicated grief. Worden, for example, recognized chronic grief, where the mourning process loses intensity over a lengthy period of time; exaggerated grief, where a particular manifestation of grief, such as anger or guilt, becomes intense and impairs functioning; delayed grief, in which the intense grief reaction occurs some time long after the original loss and is often triggered by another event such as a subsequent loss or a significant date; and masked grief, where grief underlies another presenting problem, such as substance abuse, acting out behaviors, or eating disorders.

In addition to these mental health issues, grief also can affect physical health. Several studies have indicated increased morbidity and higher mortality rates among the bereaved, especially older widows or widowers, sometimes known as the "broken heart syndrome" (see Williams, 2002.) The reasons for this increase may include the fact that many older widows and widowers have shared a lifestyle that included factors conducive to chronic disease, such as smoking, alcohol abuse, poor diet, or stress. Grief is a major stressor; grieving individuals, particularly older infirm persons, may experience health problems as a result of that stress. Finally, the death of someone, particularly a spouse, may lead to changes in health practices or lifestyle as persons may stop exercising, find it difficult to sleep, lapse into poor diets, or fail to adhere to a medical regimen.

In short, there has long been a recognition that while many individuals are relatively resilient when experiencing a loss and others may struggle with grief but ultimately navigate the transition successfully, some may find severe impairments to their physical and mental health. Thus, as the revision of the *DSM-IV-TR* approached, there were a series of recommendations that more complicated variants of grief should be acknowledged.

COMPLICATED GRIEF IN THE *DSM-5*

The demise of the bereavement exclusion

Perhaps one of the most highly debated decisions in the development of the *DSM-5* was the removal of the "bereavement exclusion" from the diagnosis of major depressive disorder. The bereavement exclusion did not exist in the first two editions of the *DSM*, nor was it ever included in the other major diagnostic tool, *The International Classification of Diseases (ICD)* (World Health Organization, 1992). The bereavement exclusion was first added to the *DSM-III* at the recommendation of one of the task force members; however, there was very limited evidence underlying the recommendation (Kendler, 2010). Studies by Clayton, Desmarais, and Winokur (1968) noted that many bereaved individuals had symptoms of a mild depression that dissipated over time without treatment and differed in a number of ways from a major depressive episode. Clayton (2010) cautioned against overdiagnosing depression in the first year. In fact, one of the reasons the *DSM-III* introduced the exclusion was to counter the common medical treatment of acute grief, particularly by primary care physicians who simply offered antidepressive medications to patients who were having normal, albeit painful, reactions to loss. Originally the bereavement exclusion was for the first year after a loss, but that was reduced to 2 months in the *DSM-IV*.

The decision to drop the bereavement exclusion altogether in the *DSM-5* created a firestorm of controversy. The Association for Death Education and Counseling (ADEC) recommended in 2012 that the bereavement exclusion not be removed. In 2013, another group of grief scholars in the International Work Group on Death, Dying, and Bereavement also issued a paper opposing elimination of the exclusion. The arguments for retaining the bereavement exclusion noted that in many ways the early manifestations of grief were difficult to differentiate from depression, especially by primary care physicians who would be far more likely to prescribe antidepressants. There was a concern then that such treatment had little evidence basis and, in fact, might distort the normal process of adjusting to a loss while also creating a harmful dependence on antidepressants. Underlying this was a fear by groups such as ADEC that the pharmaceutical industry was behind or welcomed this change to gain access to a much larger market. In summation, the arguments against the elimination of the bereavement exclusion suggested that mild depression is a common manifestation of grief and there could be a danger of overdiagnosing depression and overmedicating the grieving patient.

The arguments for eliminating the bereavement exclusion were equally as compelling. As stated earlier, such exclusion was not present in two previous editions of the *DSM* nor was it ever in the *ICD*. Moreover, neither the inclusion of the bereavement exclusion in the *DSM-III* nor its modification in the *DSM-IV* had a firm evidentiary basis.

To many professionals, the exclusion seemed illogical. One, after all, could be diagnosed with depression after a number of adverse events. Thus, one could be diagnosed with major depressive disorder after a job loss, divorce, or traumatic physical experience, but not for living through the death of a spouse, parent, or child. Following that logic, the argument could be made that a depressive response to any adverse circumstance should be excluded. Such a widespread exclusion in the definition would make the diagnosis of a major depressive disorder almost meaningless and would not be supported by research (Kendler, 2010).

The argument was also made by ADEC that a diagnosis of a major depressive disorder does not necessarily lead to pharmaceutical intervention. As Kendler (2010) notes, watchful waiting is often a sound strategy in medical treatment. A urologist may not remove an enlarged prostate or begin immediate medical treatment, waiting instead to see if it progresses to a malignant phase or impairs urological functioning. When treating someone who is grieving, a psychiatrist or family physician might wait to see if other factors, such as suicidal ideation, significant impairment in key roles, or worsening depression, would make medication necessary.

In its final publication, the *DSM-5* removed the bereavement exclusion from the diagnosis of a major depressive disorder. However, the authors of the new edition did caution that responses to a loss, as well as other adverse circumstances, may include some of the criteria associated with depression, such as weight loss, insomnia, rumination, or poor appetite. In addition, in an extensive footnote, the *DSM-5* carefully outlined that while in grief the prevailing affect is one of emptiness, in major depressive disorder it is a long-sustained depressed mood and an inability to ever expect pleasure or happiness. Moreover, the *DSM-5* notes that grief typically comes in waves that lessen in intensity and frequency over time, while a depressed mood is more persistent. Furthermore, even in grief, bereaved individuals may experience moments of positive feelings, including humor, that are generally not found in depression. The *DSM-5* also states that bereaved individuals are likely to retain feelings of self-worth and self-esteem generally not present in depression. Finally, the *DSM-5* affirms that while symptoms such as suicidal or negative ideation can occur in grief, they are generally focused on the deceased. For example, a bereaved individual may wish to "join" the deceased, or feel guilty about any significant omissions or commissions in their relationship, such as failure to visit more often or having said something unkind to the deceased. In depression, these feelings are more likely directed at self; the individual is likely to feel worthless and any suicidal ideation arises either from that feeling or from the inability to cope with the challenges faced or the pain experienced.

As of the writing of this chapter, it appears that the dire consequences predicted by opponents of the change have not yet appeared. There do not seem to be any commercials from pharmaceutical companies urging bereaved individuals to seek or discuss medications with their physicians, and no evidence exists of a significant increase in prescriptions for antidepressants. Yet, careful studies in the future will need to assess whether this change will help or hinder support for the bereaved.

Other changes in the DSM-5

Perhaps the least controversial decision was to continue to include bereavement as a V-code which lists "other conditions that might be the focus of clinical attention." Such a continuation simply acknowledges that individuals may need to seek grief counseling as they cope with a significant loss.

Two other changes were also relatively noncontroversial. The *DSM-5* removed the exclusion of grief from adjustment disorders. Adjustment disorders are defined as a response to a stressing life change, such as divorce or death, that seems out of proportion to the event itself beyond the culturally expected norm, and impairs the individual's ability to function in key educational, social, occupational, familial, or other important roles. Again, this specific change recognizes that such symptoms are beyond the cultural expectations of normal bereavement.

A second change was to allow separation anxiety disorder, once a diagnosis exclusively used with children and adolescents, to be applied to adults. The criteria emphasize that this is a recurring fear of separation or death that impairs the individual's ability to function in key roles. In this disorder, individuals are reluctant to leave home or attachment figures and may have nightmares with themes of separation. The *DSM-5,* while noting that these criteria should be applied with some flexibility, indicated that generally the condition should be minimally and persistently present for at least 4 weeks in children and adolescents but typically for 6 months in adults. The *DSM-5* makes the distinction that while grief involves yearning for the deceased, a specific fear of separation from other attachment figures (which may be triggered by loss) is the central factor in separation anxiety disorder.

Finally, the *DSM-5* retained the diagnosis of posttraumatic stress disorder (PTSD). This, too, may be a manifestation of complicated grief, as it can arise from witnessing or learning about a traumatic event such as a violent or sudden death. This experience can result in a series of symptoms including intrusive memories, flashbacks, or dreams, as well as other symptoms, that last longer than a month and once again impair the individual's ability to function in key roles.

Persistent complex bereavement disorder

As work commenced on the *DSM-5,* there was widespread recognition that anywhere between 7% to 20% of bereaved individuals experienced more complicated forms of grief (Middleton, Burnett, Raphael, & Martinek, 1996). Varied groups of researchers have made several attempts to characterize forms of more complicated grief disorders including traumatic grief disorder, bereavement-related disorder, pathological grief disorder, complicated grief disorder, and prolonged grief disorder.

These efforts generated some level of controversy. While there was a general recognition that grief can be complicated and that a *DSM* diagnosis would facilitate reimbursement for treatment, there was acknowledgment that a *DSM* diagnosis could perhaps pathologize grief and carry risks of both overdiagnosis and unnecessary medication. Others believed that with the removal of the bereavement exclusions for adjustment disorders and major depressive disorders, as well as the addition of allowing adults to be diagnosed with separation anxiety disorder, there was no need for a distinct diagnostic category for additional forms of complicated grief.

Ultimately, both prolonged grief disorder (Prigerson et al., 2009) and complicated grief disorder (Shear et al., 2011) seemed to generate the most interest. Yet, because the *DSM* attempts to identify a general consensus and sees itself as evidenced-based, the *DSM* panel did not incorporate either proposal. The panel did add persistent complex bereavement disorder, listed as a "candidate disorder" in Section III under the category "Conditions for Further Study." The criteria here encompassed elements of complicated grief disorder and prolonged grief disorder, as well as pathological grief disorder, that had been earlier incorporated in prolonged grief disorder (Horowitz, Bonanno, & Holen, 1993). By listing it as a candidate disorder in Section III, the reviewing committee affirmed that there is a body of evidence suggesting a form of disorder, yet not enough to fully specify the features of such a disorder. It served as a call to the field to continue research that can carefully delineate the characteristics of such a syndrome. To many, the decision to use persistent complex bereavement disorder seems to imply that the reviewing committee was unwilling to give primacy to either of the two underlying proposals.

Childhood traumatic grief disorder: An emerging condition?

Throughout the process of the revision of the *DSM-5*, there was exploration of a possible diagnosis of childhood traumatic grief disorder or developmental trauma disorder, but these were ultimately not included in the *DSM-5* as either a full diagnosis or a candidate disorder. Such a diagnosis might be given to a child or adolescent after the child or adolescent experienced a death that was perceived as terrifying or involved other losses or adversities, such as having to relocate to a new neighborhood or having to testify in a court case. In this case, the child or adolescent would have experienced a variety of intrusive symptoms and grief that interfere with his or her development and roles, while also impairing his or her ability to transcend the loss. It was further hypothesized that some children and adolescents might show extreme avoidance patterns and, if the condition was untreated, that it could result in a series of mental disorders in adulthood, such as depression, substance abuse, or eating disorders.

Such a diagnostic category faced a relatively high bar for inclusion. First, it would need to establish an evidence basis that this is a unique diagnosis in children and adolescents that was clearly separate and distinct from PTSD. Second, this diagnosis would need evidence to demonstrate that the symptoms of this disorder are distinct because of the violent and sudden way the child's parent died. Here, however, evidence has been mixed. For example, McClatchy, Vonk, and Palardy's (2009) research compared children's reactions to both sudden, unexpected loss and expected loss on childhood traumatic grief symptoms. They found no significant differences between these two groups, suggesting that parental loss,whatever the circumstances, is inherently traumatic for the child.

Though no such diagnosis was included in the *DSM-5,* it is likely that this will be a continued discussion in future revisions. It seems an anomaly that there is neither a diagnosis specific to children and adolescents who have experienced significant traumatic events that have distorted development, nor a diagnostic category specifying the unique complications (beyond attachment disorders) that grieving children and adolescents may experience as they cope with a significant loss.

CONCLUSION

This chapter reviewed the varied ways and underlying issues leading to the recognition of complicated grief within the *DSM-5.* At present, professionals acknowledge that loss can trigger depression and understand that bereavement can be a factor in adjustment disorders while also eliciting separation anxiety, even in adults. Despite speculation that the V-code might be removed for normal bereavement, it was retained. In addition, persistent complex bereavement disorder was offered as a candidate disorder pending further research and future consensus. Given that this label was suggested as a compromise, it is possible that a future revision may not use the same name to delineate a similar condition.

A number of theorists, clinicians, and researchers (Rando et. al., 2012) concur that "complicated grief is complicated." They note that a number of syndromes have been identified as possible forms of complicated grief including, but not limited to, delayed grief, distorted grief, inhibited grief, and varied forms of chronic grief. They call for continued research and possible future inclusion of other forms of complicated grief. In addition, the interest in childhood traumatic grief suggests that further research should explore the unique forms that complicated grief might take in children and adolescents, particularly in eating disorders; substance abuse and addictive disorders; and varied forms of disruptive, impulse-control, and conduct disorders.

The *DSM-5* in many ways represented a significant advance in the diagnosis and treatment of varied forms of mourning. To a certain extent, it answered Freud's challenge of nearly a century ago to distinguish mourning and melancholia, differentiating normal grief from depression. Most importantly, it took the first significant, albeit small, steps to acknowledge complications in the grief process. Yet, the discussion and debate that ensued indicate that far more needs to be done.

Author's Note: One of the most apparent changes in the *DSM* was to move from Roman numerals to Arabic numbers. This change will allow minor revisions listed as 5.1, 5.2, etc., prior to the release of a major revision that would be listed as *DSM-6*. This is significant, as it implies recognition of the fact that understanding and classifying mental disorders is likely to continually change with new and ongoing research.

Kenneth J. Doka, PhD, MDiv, is a professor of gerontology at the Graduate School of The College of New Rochelle and senior consultant to Hospice Foundation of America. Dr. Doka serves as editor of HFA's Living with Grief® *book series, its* Journeys *newsletter, and numerous other books and publications. Dr. Doka has served as a panelist on HFA's* Living with Grief® *video programs for 24 years. He is a past president of the Association for Death Education and Counseling (ADEC) and received their Special Contributions Award in the field of Death Education. He is a member and past chair of the International Work Group on Death, Dying, and Bereavement. In 2006, Dr. Doka was grandfathered in as a mental health counselor under New York's first state licensure of counselors. Dr. Doka is an ordained Lutheran minister.*

REFERENCES

American Psychiatric Association. (2000). *Diagnostic and statistical manual of mental disorders* (4th ed., rev.). *DSM-IV-TR*. Washington, DC: American Psychiatric Association.

American Psychiatric Association. (2013). *Diagnostic and statistical manual of mental disorders* (5th ed.). Washington, DC: American Psychiatric Association.

Clayton, P., Desmarais, L. & Winokur, G. (1968). A study of normal bereavement. *American Journal of Psychiatry, 125,* 168-178.

Clayton, P. (2010). V-code for bereavement. *Journal of Clinical Psychiatry, 7,* 359-360.

Deutsch, H. (1937). Absence of grief. *Psychoanalytic Quarterly, 6,* 12-22.

Doka, K. J. (Ed.). (1989). *Disenfranchised grief: Recognizing hidden sorrow.* Lexington, MA: Lexington Books.

Doka, K. J. (Ed). (2002). *Disenfranchised grief: New directions, challenges and strategies for practice.* Champaign, IL: Research Press.

Freud, S. (1917/1957). Mourning and melancholia. In J. Strachey (Ed.), *The standard edition of the complete psychological works of Sigmund Freud* (Vol. 14, pp. 237-260). London, UK: Hogarth Press.

Horowitz, M. J., Bonanno, G. A., & Holen, A. (1993). Pathological grief: Diagnosis and explanation. *Psychosomatic Medicine, 55,* 260-273.

Kendler, K. (2010). Grief exclusion. Paper published by the American Psychiatric Association. http://www.dsm5.org/about/Documents/grief%20exclusion_Kendler.pdf

Lindemann, E. (1944). Symptomatology and management of acute grief. *American Journal of Psychiatry, 101*(3), 141-149.

McClatchy, I., Vonk, M., & Palardy, G. (2009). The prevalence of childhood traumatic grief: A comparison of violent/sudden and expected loss. *OMEGA—Journal of Death and Dying, 59,* 305-323.

Middleton, W., Burnett, P., Raphael, B., & Martinek, N. (1996). The bereavement response: A cluster analysis. *The British Journal of Psychiatry, 169*(2), 167-171.

Prigerson, H. G., Horowitz, M. J., Jacobs, S. C., Parkes, C. M., Aslan, M., Goodkin, K.,...Maciejewski, P. K. (2009). Prolonged grief disorder: Psychometric validation of criteria proposed for DSM-V and ICD-11. *PLoS Medicine, 6*(8), e1000121

Rando, T. A. (1993). *Treatment of complicated mourning.* Champaign, IL: Research Press.

Rando, T. A., Doka, K. J., Fleming, S., Franco, M. H., Lobb, A., Parkes, C. M., & Steele, R. (2012). A call to the field: Complicated grief in the *DSM-5. OMEGA—Journal of Death and Dying, 65,* 251-255.

Shand, A. F. (1914). *The foundation of character.* London, UK: Macmillan.

Shear, M. K., Simon, N., Wall, M., Zisook, S., Neimeyer, R., Duan, N.,...Keshaviah, A. (2011). Complicated grief and related bereavement issues for DSM-5. *Depression and Anxiety, 28*(2), 103-117.

Stroebe, M., Hansson, R., Schut, H., & Stroebe, W. (2008). *Handbook of bereavement research and practice: Advances in theory and intervention.* Washington, DC: American Psychological Association.

Williams, J. R. (2002). Effects of grief on survivor's health. In K. J. Doka (Ed.). *Living with grief: Loss in later life* (pp. 191-206). Washington, DC: Hospice Foundation of America.

Worden, J. W. (2009). *Grief counseling and grief therapy* (4th ed.). New York, NY: Springer.

World Health Organization. (1992). *The ICD-10 classification of mental and behavioural disorders: Clinical descriptions and diagnostic guidelines.* Geneva: World Health Organization.

Forms of Complicated Grief

J. William Worden

Ever since Freud wrote his classic book *Mourning and Melancholia* (1917), clinicians have been thinking about what makes grief and mourning complicated. Freud made a distinction between the mourning process and melancholia, a term that refers to depression. In his early work, Freud, along with his colleague Abraham (1927), focused on specific behavioral characteristics that made grief abnormal and distinct from depression. These behaviors included (a) episodes of panic, (b) hostility toward the self, (c) regression to a narcissistic preoccupation, and (d) other signs of deflated self-esteem. When these behaviors were present, Freud defined the person's grief as being "abnormal." However, more current research in bereavement has shown that these same characteristics outlined by Freud can be found in a random sample of normal mourners.

When Eric Lindemann, former head of psychiatry at the Massachusetts General Hospital, studied the experiences of persons bereaved by the death of loved ones in the 1942 Boston Cocoanut Grove nightclub fire, he focused primarily on describing characteristics of the normal grief experience (1944). However, the data in some of his cases looked very much like what contemporary clinicians would call complicated bereavement. A renewed interest in complicated mourning came about upon the publication of *Grief Counseling and Grief Therapy* (Worden, 1982). In this book, I outlined four types of complicated bereavement and showed how they could be both diagnosed and treated. This interest in grief and mourning was stimulated by the work of Colin Murray Parkes who, in the 1960s and 70s, was investigator of the Harvard Bereavement Study, a study investigating the experiences of young widows and widowers in the Boston area.

Following the publication of my book, there was an upsurge of interest in complicated mourning in the next decade. Beverley Raphael and her colleagues in Australia sent out a questionnaire to clinicians working in the area of grief and bereavement asking them which categories of complicated bereavement they used in their practice. This format was an unusual way to establish clinical categories, looking at their popularity rather than examining which categories can be validated through empirical investigation. After Raphael published the results of her questionnaire, three other grief investigators published books outlining categories of complicated mourning (Sanders,1989; Rando, 1993; Jacobs, 1993).

A common thread in these works was the use of two categories: chronic grief and delayed grief. In addition, one or more of these writers suggested categories, such as exaggerated/distorted grief, masked grief, and inhibited or absent grief. Rando added two other categories, unanticipated grief and conflicted grief, to the list. The table below shows categories of complicated bereavement popular in the years 1982 through 1993.

Categories of Complicated Bereavement in Academic Literature (1982 – 1993)

	Worden 1982	Raphael 1983	Sanders 1989	Rando 1993	Jacobs 1993
Chronic (C)	C	C	C	C	C
Delayed (D)	D	D	D	D	D
Exaggerated (E)/ Distorted (Di)	E, Di	E, Di	Di	Di	Di
Masked (M)/ Inhibited (I)/ Absent (A)	M	I	--	A, I	I
Unanticipated (U)	--	--	--	U	--
Conflicted (Co)	--	--	--	Co	--

In 1995, Holly Prigerson and her colleagues at the University of Pittsburgh set about to define a category of complicated bereavement that would be sufficiently vigorous to find a place in the next *Diagnostic and Statistical Manual of Mental Disorders (DSM)* of the American Psychiatric Association (APA). In previous versions of the *DSM*, grief reactions were only found as a V-code, one that does not allow for reimbursement. Prigerson and her colleagues originally called this disorder traumatic grief; they later changed the name to complicated grief and still later to prolonged grief.

Prigerson and her colleagues had three goals: to establish a clinical entity called complicated grief; to identify those having complicated grief who would be at risk for long-term dysfunction (social, psychological, and medical); and to distinguish complicated grief from bereavement related to depression and anxiety. When the *DSM-5* was published in 2013, Prigerson's category was not included in the main section of the manual but was, somewhat modified, listed in Section III as persistent complex bereavement disorder in the list of "Conditions for Further Study" (APA).

Another change between editions of the *DSM* was the removal of the bereavement exclusion. In the *DSM-IV* there had been a 3-month period before bereaved individuals could receive a diagnosis of depression (APA, 1994). In the *DSM-5* this exclusion was dropped, making a major depressive episode available as a diagnostic category for newly-bereaved individuals (APA, 2013).

FOUR TYPES OF COMPLICATED MOURNING

This definition of complicated bereavement is one that has helped to shape a current paradigm that outlines four types of complicated mourning and is the one I prefer:

> Complicated bereavement is the intensification of grief to the level where the person is overwhelmed, resorts to maladaptive behavior, or remains interminably in the state of grief without progression of the mourning toward completion. In normal grief, the transition, however painful, is neither overwhelmingly interminable nor prematurely interrupted (Worden, 2009).

The strength of this definition is the exclusion of pain as a determining factor. A mourner may be experiencing a great deal of pain but that does not indicate that he or she is experiencing complicated mourning. The case examples below help to clarify these four categories.

Chronic grief

Chronic grief is a form of complicated bereavement that was noted as a category used by all of the therapists and investigators in the Raphael study. It is also the focus of Prigerson in her investigations as well as those of Katherine Shear. Shear has done much in her research and clinical interventions to enhance an understanding of chronic or prolonged grief (Shear et al., 2005a, 2005b). In chronic grief the mourning process is prolonged and over time does not move toward some kind of resolution. Clinicians argue about the length of time since the death that makes this type of mourning complicated, as it is accepted overall that the mourning process can be quite prolonged in a normal mourner. Many clinicians, including myself, believe that chronic grief should not be diagnosed within the first year after a death. If someone comes to a therapist 6 months after the death of a loved one saying that they have chronic grief, they may need education about the grief process. Many are having experiences that they have never had before, and the counselor can help normalize what they are experiencing.

In my clinical experience, chronic grief is usually self-diagnosed by the client. Clients come 2, 3, or 5 years after a death and frequently present by saying, "I'm not getting over this," "I'm not doing what I did before my loved one died," or "I'm feeling stuck." This self-diagnosis is usually quite valid, and the task of the therapist is to discover, with the patient's help, how they are stuck and then deal with whatever conflicts of separation are causing the problem. The therapist needs to use a theoretical model that explains the mourning process and serves as an anchor for his or her interventions. Many therapists find that the Task Model that I have developed is useful in discovering the point or points of "stuckness." Other models that can be helpful for use with a patient experiencing chronic grief are the Six R-model of Rando (1993), the Two Track model of Rubin (1981, 1999), the Dual Process model of Stroebe and Schut (1999), and the Meaning Making model of Neimeyer (2001).

Case example

Jane's son died in a midair plane collision; his body was never retrieved, and it happened far away from where she lived. Two years after his death, Jane shared with her minister: "I'm not getting over this. I'm not doing the things that I did before my son died and I need some help." The minister referred her to me. I began the grief therapy by asking, "Tell me about your son, since I didn't know him." As she told me about Tony, he came off as the greatest son who ever lived; he had been a high-ranking military cadet and a top student at an Ivy League school. Often when a lost loved one is presented to the therapist as bigger than life, the mourner is overstating all the good parts of the person in order to escape some of the ambivalence existing in the relationship. The role of the therapist at this point is to encourage the positive characteristics being presented by the mourner; as therapy progresses, one can explore with the client more mixed characteristics that may have engendered disappointment and resentment.

After a few sessions, Jane shared that about 30 days before Tony was killed he had done something that had severely displeased her. The situation between them was not resolved before the accident, so all of her anger and disappointment was suppressed. The goal of this therapy became to help Jane express her negative feelings and disappointments to her son and to see that these negative thoughts and feelings would not take away all of her positive memories. Moving forward comes as the patient finds the balance between the positive and negative remembrances and feelings. In a follow-up with Jane, she told me, "I am doing fine. I am now doing all the things I didn't do when my son died."

One technique that is useful in this kind of therapy is having the patient speak directly to his or her lost loved one in an "empty chair;" this technique was often used in Gestalt therapy (Polster & Polster, 1973; Field & Horowitz, 1998). There is more power in *talking to* the person than in *talking about* the person to the therapist. If a patient does not want to talk to an empty chair, ask them to close their eyes and imagine that they are talking to their lost loved one. The process of talking to the dead loved one usually elicits a great deal of affect that the therapist can help sanction and direct. A word of caution: this technique is not one to be used with a borderline patient whose boundaries are not well-defined and who may not know where he or she ends and the other person begins. However, most patients can handle this technique well and it helps them deal with the unfinished business between themselves and their loved one. Compliance improves when the counselor believes in the process and can project this confidence to the client.

Would a patient like Jane have made progress without getting some kind of specialized treatment? I don't think so. Most patients with chronic grief have been struggling for several years with the conflict without seeing any resolution. A knowledgeable therapist can rather quickly help the patient identify the conflicts of separation that preclude them from moving forward with their mourning and help them find some movement. The Zeigarnik principle says that "an unfinished task is remembered longer than a completed task" (Wheeler, 1991). These conflicts of separation tend to live at a low level of awareness in the patient. An experienced therapist can help bring these conflicts into a more conscious awareness and facilitate them toward closure.

Delayed grief

The second type of complicated bereavement is delayed grief. In delayed grief the mourner may have had some kind of grief reaction after the death, but for one reason or another it was not sufficient. Many times this situation is due to a lack of social support. Because the grief is delayed, a later event or smaller loss can trigger a large grief response. The grieving person knows that the mourning for this loss is excessive but may not be able to identify the earlier loss from which some of this excessive grief stems. In my practice, I've frequently seen this when a person is going through a divorce, when experiencing the loss of a pet, or even when someone has an excessive response to a movie or television program. I've also seen it in people who volunteer as hospice workers, where their work with a current hospice patient may re-evoke grief from an earlier personal loss. Most of the time the mourner realizes that his grief response far exceeds what might be expected from these lesser losses.

Sometimes a delayed grief response comes up in a regular counseling or therapy session. The client exhibits sad affect even though he or she may be dealing with another issue not specifically related to loss or sadness. When this sadness comes up spontaneously in the therapy session, it is important that the therapist encourage the patient not to cut the sadness but to stay with it. Following the sadness over an "affective bridge" can lead to something trying to emerge into awareness, frequently an earlier loss that was inadequately mourned. Another way to identify delayed grief is by listening to themes coming up in a therapy session. Themes of grief and loss can be brought to the client's awareness and be explored to see if these earlier losses still need to be mourned.

The treatment is fairly straightforward. Once the client and the therapist have identified the earlier loss that may be triggering the current sadness, the therapist can encourage the patient to experience the grief from the original loss and can provide the social support that may have been lacking at the time of the earlier loss.

Case example

In a weekly therapy group that focused mostly on personal growth, Maria shared that she was very upset that her best friend had lost a baby 6 months into her pregnancy. Members of the therapy group rallied around to support her, but her distress continued over the next several weeks of group meetings. I became concerned that Maria was mourning the dead baby perhaps even more than her friend, the birth mother, and began to suspect that this may have had something to do with her own loss history. I asked Maria privately and she shared that as a college student she became pregnant and then had terminated the pregnancy; no one knew about the pregnancy or its termination, not the man involved or her family. She did not mourn her own loss and proceeded to put it out of mind. Yet, her own grief began to surface as she was confronted by her friend's loss. Maria decided to share her experience with the group. The members supported her, and this support helped her mourn the loss of her own child, who she was able to talk to using the empty chair technique.

In delayed grief, which is sometimes called inhibited grief or suppressed grief, it is important to remember that the person may have done some grieving at the time of the original loss, but it was not sufficient. For various reasons, this grief gets reactivated as part of a later loss event. Once the original loss is identified, it is fairly easy to encourage the person to do the grief work needed to move forward. However, intense grieving for an earlier loss can be awkward for some clients. A friend or colleague may notice the sadness and ask, "For whom are you grieving?" The griever says, "For my father;" but if the father died 10 years earlier, this can potentially be an awkward situation and the client may need help as how to handle this.

Exaggerated grief

This category may not appear in everyone's nomenclature of complicated mourning, but it is, in my opinion, an important addition. Exaggerated grief means that the person is having an experience normal to most mourners, but the experience is exaggerated to the point that he or she is experiencing dysfunctional behavior. For example, it is normal for the mourner to experience sadness, even deep sadness. But if the sadness is exaggerated to the point of a major depressive episode, then I would include this under exaggerated grief. It is normal for many mourners to feel anxious after losing a loved one. But if this anxiety is exacerbated to the point of an anxiety disorder, then I would put it under exaggerated grief.

The question arises whether this category is even necessary; most of the symptoms being experienced by the mourner can be found in the *DSM-5* in the diagnoses of anxiety disorders, depressive disorders, obsessive-compulsive disorders, substance abuse, and posttraumatic stress disorder. The reasons for keeping exaggerated grief as a category are (a) most of the mourners experiencing these disorders have not experienced such symptoms before; (b) they can readily associate the beginning of the symptoms with a recent loss they have experienced; and (c) once the disorder is cured, they may never again experience a similar set of symptoms.

The treatment for these disorders is the same as they would be when treating the disorders in a nonbereaved person, but the differences lie in the direction of treatment. After the symptoms begin to abate, often through the use of medication, then the "conflicts of separation" can be dealt with in the therapy.

Case example

Gail, a woman in her early forties, became severely depressed after the death of her father. She had not experienced any prior episodes of depression, but after her father's death her depression was so severe that her husband would find her curled up in a fetal position in the backyard. She was referred to me for treatment, which we began with a course of antidepressant medication. After a few weeks the depression began to lift, enabling us then to deal with the conflicts of separation. Her father had managed a successful community hospital and did not spend much time at home while she was growing up. When he was not working, he was out on the golf course. Gail remembered that as a child she would feign illness in order to get admitted to her father's hospital so she could be close to her father. As her father lay dying, Gail informed her siblings that she was the best one to care for her father; they really didn't need to be in attendance. These behaviors illustrate the intensely ambivalent relationship between Gail and her father. Once we identified this ambivalence, we could work on it in therapy sessions where she could express many thoughts and feelings that she had suppressed over the years. Gail made progress in our office sessions; to complete the treatment she went to the gravesite and addressed her father directly. Several follow-ups with her over 2 years indicated that she has had no further depressive episodes. This pattern, where someone who had no history of depression prior to a loss but experiences a significant depression that can then be helped with treatment, is common in exaggerated grief responses.

When considering this category, it is important to note that the patient is conscious that the symptom appeared after the death of a loved one, but the excessive response causes dysfunctional behavior. A whole host of standardized treatments can be invoked, such as the use of medication, cognitive behavioral interventions, and hypnosis. But keep in mind that there is a dimension of the attachment relationship and its subsequent separation that is feeding into the behavioral symptoms. Once the dysfunctional symptoms abate, then these conflicts can be addressed.

Masked grief

Masked grief is sometimes called inhibited grief or absent grief. Deutsch first identified this category in her classic paper on absent grief (1937). This category was also identified by a number of the responders to Raphael's questionnaire. In masked grief the conflicts of separation experienced by the patient are experienced either as some kind of physical symptom, psychiatric symptom, or maladaptive behavior. Unlike exaggerated grief, where the patient identifies his or her symptoms with the death of a loved one, in masked grief the patient does not recognize that the symptoms that he or she is experiencing are related to a loss. Patients experiencing these physical symptoms often go to a physician for a diagnosis and treatment. When the physician can find nothing organically wrong with the patient, a diagnosis of somatoform disorder is made, and the patient is referred to a professional for psychological help.

Case example

Fred's wife died suddenly while walking their dog. Soon after the funeral, Fred began to experience a radiating pain down his left arm. His children urged him to see his physician, who could find nothing physically wrong with him. The doctor helped Fred to see the parallel between his experience of pain and the pain that his wife had experienced and referred him to me. In treatment we began to deal with his excessive anger at his wife for leaving him so suddenly. After a few sessions, his experience of these somatic symptoms decreased and finally abated.

Zisook and DeVaul (1976) write about facsimile illness, where the patient experiences manifestations of the illness that took his or her loved one and how pain can be a symbol for felt grief. It is important that physicians include, as a part of their intake, questions about experiences with death and losses, particularly recent deaths and losses.

Physical symptoms may not be only manifestations of repressed or masked grief. The grief may also be masked as a psychiatric symptom, such as unexplained depression, or as some type of acting out or other maladaptive psychological behavior. Randall (1993) describes the case of a woman who developed anorexia nervosa 4 months after the accidental death of her son, with whom she had an overly dependent attachment. Since the age of 12, this son had had an eating disorder, for which he was hospitalized. Her introjection of her son's pathology was identified, and through the skilled use of linking objects, the therapist could help her appropriately disengage from him and master her eating disorder.

The four forms of complicated bereavement listed above can frequently be seen in the therapist's office. Other chapters in this book address specific risk factors that may lead to these types of complications as well as other intervention strategies for treating complicated grief. In much of our work as therapists with issues other than bereavement, we think that we are helping clients and certainly hope that we are. However, when we work with situations where grief may be complicated, the changes experienced by clients can be so dramatic that we know for sure our interventions are making a difference.

Author's Note: Some of this material has previously been presented in earlier editions of *Grief counseling and grief therapy: A handbook for the mental health practitioner* (Worden, 1982, 2009).

J. William Worden, PhD, ABPP, is a Fellow of the American Psychological Association and holds academic appointments at the Harvard Medical School and at the Rosemead Graduate School of Psychology in California. He is also Co-Principal Investigator of the

Harvard Child Bereavement Study, based at the Massachusetts General Hospital. Recipient of five major National Institutes of Health grants, his research and clinical work over 40 years has centered on issues of life-threatening illness and life-threatening behavior. His professional interests led him to become a founding member of the Association of Death Education and Counseling and the International Work Group on Death, Dying, and Bereavement. Worden is the author of Personal Death Awareness *and* Children & Grief: When a Parent Dies, *and is coauthor of* Helping Cancer Patients Cope. *His book* Grief Counseling & Grief Therapy: A Handbook for the Mental Health Practitioner, *now in its fourth edition, has been translated into 14 foreign languages and is widely used around the world as the standard reference on the subject.*

REFERENCES

Abraham, K. (1927). *Selected papers on psychoanalysis.* London, UK: Hogarth.

American Psychiatric Association. (2013). *Diagnostic and statistical manual of mental disorders* (5th ed.; *DSM-5*). Washington, DC: American Psychiatric Association.

American Psychiatric Association. (1994). *Diagnostic and statistical manual of mental disorders* (4th ed.; *DSM-IV*). Washington, DC: American Psychiatric Association.

Deutsch, H. (1937). Absence of grief. *Psychoanalytic Quarterly*, 6, 12-22.

Field, N., & Horowitz, M. (1998). Applying an empty-chair monologue paradigm to examine unresolved grief. *Psychiatry Interpersonal & Biological Processes*, 61, 279-287.

Freud, S. (1917/1957). Mourning and melancholia. In J. Strachey (Ed.), *The standard edition of the complete psychological works of Sigmund Freud* (Vol. 14, pp. 237-260). London, UK: Hogarth Press.

Jacobs, S. (1993.) *Pathological grief: Maladaption to loss.* Washington, DC: American Psychiatric Press.

Lazare, A. (1989). Bereavement and unresolved grief. In A. Lazare (Ed.), *Outpatient Psychiatry: Diagnosis and Treatment*, 2nd ed. (pp. 381-397). Baltimore, MD: Williams & Wilkins.

Lindemann, E. (1944). Symptomatology and management of acute grief. *American Journal of Psychiatry, 151* (6 Suppl), 155-160.

Neimeyer, R. (Ed.). (2001). *Meaning reconstruction and the experience of loss.* Washington, DC: American Psychological Association.

Parkes, C. M. (1972). *Bereavement: Studies of grief in adult life.* New York, NY: International Universities Press.

Polster, E. & Polster, M. (1973). *Gestalt therapy integrated.* New York, NY: Brunner/Mazel.

Prigerson, H. & Maciejewski, P. (2006). A call for sound empirical testing and evaluation of criteria for complicated grief proposed for DSM-V. *OMEGA—Journal of Death and Dying, 52,* 9-19.

Prigerson, H., Frank, E., Kasi, S. V., Reynolds, C. F., et al. (1995). Complicated grief and bereavemen-related depression as distinct disorders: Preliminary empirical validation in elderly bereaved spouses. *American Journal of Psychiatry, 152,* 22-30.

Prigerson, H., Bierhals, A., Kasl, S. V., Shear, M. K., Newsom, J. T., & Jacobs, S. (1996). Complicated grief as a disorder distinct from bereavement-related depression and anxiety: A replication study. *American Journal of Psychiatry, 153,* 1484-1486.

Prigerson, H., Shear, M. K., Jacobs, S. C., Reynolds, C. F., III, Maciejewski, P., Davidson, J. R.,...Zisook, S. (1999). Consensus criteria for traumatic grief: A preliminary empirical test. *British Journal of Psychiatry, 174,* 67-73.

Randall, L. (1993), Abnormal grief and eating disorders within a mother-son dyad. *British Journal of Medical Psychology, 66*: 89–96. doi:10.1111/j.2044-8341.1993.tb01730.x

Rando, T. A. (1993). *Treatment of complicated mourning.* Champaign, IL: Research Press.

Raphael, B. (1983). *The anatomy of bereavement.* New York, NY: Basic Books.

Rubin, S. S. (1981). A two-track model of bereavement: Theory and application in research. *American Journal of Orthopsychiatry, 5,* 101-109.

Rubin, S. S. (1999). The two-track model of bereavement: Overview, retrospect, and prospect. *Death Studies, 23*, 681-714.

Sanders, C. M. (1989). Grief: The mourning after. New York, NY: Wiley.

Shear, K., & Shair, H. (2005a). Attachment, loss, and complicated grief. *Developmental Psychobiology, 47*, 253-267.

Shear, K., Frank, E., Houck, P. R., & Reynolds, C. F. (2005b). Treatment of complicated grief: A randomized controlled trial. *JAMA, 293*, 2601-2608.

Stroebe, M. S., & Schut, H. (1999). The Dual Process Model of coping with bereavement: Rationale and description. *Death Studies, 23*, 197-224.

Wheeler, G. (1991). *Gestalt reconsidered: A new approach to contact and resistance*. New York, NY: GIC Press.

Worden, J. W. (1982). *Grief counseling and grief therapy: A handbook for the mental health practitioner*. New York, NY: Springer.

Worden, J. W. (2009). *Grief counseling and grief therapy: A handbook for the mental health practitioner (4th Ed.)*. New York, NY: Springer.

Zisook, S., & DeVaul, R. A. (1976). Grief-related facsimile illness. *International Journal of Psychiatry Medicine, 7*, 329-336.

Zisook, S., & Kendler, K. S. (2007). Is bereavement-related depression different than non-bereavement-related depression? *Psychological Medicine, 37*, 779-794.

Zisook, S., Corruble, E., Duan, N., Iglewicz, A., Karam, E. G., Lanuoette, N.,...Young, I. T. (2012). The bereavement exclusion and DSM-5. *Depression & Anxiety, 29*, 425-443.

CHAPTER 3

When Grief Disables

Nancy Boyd Webb

As the readers of this volume well know, every death is different, and the responses of different individuals to a death vary widely, even within the same family. The grieving process takes many forms and can run the gamut from devastating to transformational. Grief that overwhelms and incapacitates a person has been referred to as disabling (Webb, 1993; 2002; 2010; Helping Hand, 2012). The length of time and the extent of the disabling condition varies and determines whether the reaction qualifies as complicated. Most of the chapters in this book refer to the presence of disabling factors that contribute to the overall diagnosis of complicated grief; disabling grief is an integral component, even central element, of complicated grief.

This chapter will review the various elements that can contribute to making grief disabling. Case examples will highlight the diverse influences that, in combination, can cause an individual to become dysfunctional after a death. Appropriate assessment of the grieving person is an important step toward providing treatment options that can help the mourner overcome the impasse of disabling grief and return to his or her previous level of functioning.

VARIOUS BEREAVEMENT RESPONSES AND DIAGNOSES

The terminology associated with bereavement is continually evolving. In attempting to understand and describe an individual's grief response, counselors may consider many potential diagnoses or categories. The possible choices include: persistent complex bereavement disorder, complicated grief, pathological grief, traumatic grief, major depressive episode (MDE), and posttraumatic stress disorder (PTSD) (Jordan & Litz, 2014; American Psychiatric Association [APA], 2013; Prigerson et al., 2009). Although these distinctions are familiar to grief counselors, only MDE and PTSD are listed in the fifth edition of the *Diagnostic and Statistical Manual of Mental Disorders* (5th ed.; *DSM-5*; APA, 2013), the guiding resource on which mental health professionals rely for diagnoses. Persistent complex bereavement disorder appears in Section III under the category of "Conditions for Further Study" as a possible diagnosis awaiting confirmation of validity (APA, 2013). The group of experts that determined what to include in the *DSM-5* has been cautious about designating grief responses as mental disorders. In contrast, the diagnoses of MDE and PTSD have a longer history of being included in the manual and have been studied and validated using empirical research.

Disabling grief

The term disabling grief is not a separate, distinct diagnosis in the *DSM-5*. Yet, the characteristics of impaired or disabled functioning appear as universal elements in the other diagnoses associated with complicated bereavement. There is a great deal of overlap among the diagnoses mentioned above. Virtually all of them include the presence of feelings of helplessness and reduced ability to function as factors used in determining each diagnosis. Because of the ever-present disabling component in the various bereavement and depressive diagnoses, practitioners must be aware of the universality and influence of different degrees of disability as a common element in grief. This chapter will review this disabling component in its various forms and presentations to better understand how this response impacts individuals of all ages, making them feel hopeless and helpless as they struggle with their grief.

In my book *Helping Bereaved Children* (Webb, 1993; 2002; 2010), I used disabling grief to describe a cluster of grief reactions that interfere with a child's normal developmental course. My intent was to avoid terms such as unresolved grief or delayed grief, which might lead family members and counselors to assume that the symptoms would repair themselves in time and that the child could "work things out" per his or her individual needs and schedule. The concept of disabling grief was welcomed by many therapists who wanted to assist a bereaved child floundering in the throes of bereavement crosscurrents. The concept permits consideration of the use of certain remedial and therapeutic methods, such as lending support to help the person tolerate his or her uncomfortable feelings. We know that adults, as well as children, experience disabling grief; therefore, the concept applies to all persons who have become unable to carry on with their usual activities following the death of someone who was significant in their lives.

Responses to loss

Most deaths bring about feelings of loss and deprivation to close survivors, and these responses can be mild, moderate, or severe. Much depends on the nature of the relationship and the type and degree of attachment between the deceased and the survivor. When the person who died was a beloved family member or friend who played a consistent and significant role in the life of the mourner, it is quite understandable that the loss would bring with it strong feelings of deprivation. A loss of this kind combines the absence of not only an important attachment figure, but also the beneficial functions this person provided to the survivor as well as to the circle of other surviving friends and relatives. Examples of these functions include that of breadwinner, cook, caretaker, or family peacemaker—any of the countless roles that people typically take for granted until they are confronted with the death of the individual who routinely fulfilled these functions.

Responses to a death may be immediate or delayed, and they may cause different degrees of impact on the survivor's ability to carry on with his or her usual life activities. This impact is influenced by the degree of intrusiveness into the survivor's life created by the grieving process. If physical development shows signs of impairment, his or her grief process can justifiably be considered disabling; the deliberate use of the term indicates an acknowledgment that something is definitely wrong. The terms disabling, delayed, and complicated grief all refer to a person's negative adjustment to a bereavement loss that may signal a need for intervention. Although the proposed criteria for a disorder of complicated grief is not applicable until 6 months after the death and the proposed criteria for prolonged grief disorder is after 18 months (Bonanno et al., 2002), my view is that counselors should offer support whenever necessary.

Intervention Recommendations

The use of play therapy in disabling grief (Susan, age 9)

This case was initially published in the first edition of *Helping Bereaved Children* (Webb, 1993) and is presented here in a shortened version to demonstrate the nature of a child's disabling responses after a close friend's tragic death and how play therapy helped to reduce the girl's anxiety and distress.

Susan was referred to me 4 weeks after her best friend died in a terrible car accident. The young boy died instantly when the car went off the road, and the rumor was that he had been decapitated. Susan was having nightmares and headaches, was irritable, and was keeping more to herself than prior to her friend's death. Her affect was constricted as demonstrated in the fact that she did not cry at the funeral, and she refused to enter her friend's house when her mother went to visit the grieving family. The diagnosis that most closely reflected Susan's symptoms was PTSD. I treated Susan with short-term play therapy, which resulted in relief of her symptoms after seven sessions.

Disabling factors

Susan's mother primarily sought counseling for Susan because her nightly waking with nightmares caused her mother to be concerned. The fact that Susan had repressed her feelings of grief over her friend's death resulted in these fears and anxieties erupting in her dreams that involved a monster chasing her. Sleep disturbances are a frequent disabling response for children who are grieving. They are afraid and unable to express their feelings directly in words, resulting in these fears emerging in a disguised and frightening manner in their sleep. The fact that Susan was having headaches in school was another disabling factor that, if left unnoticed or untreated, could have caused her school work to suffer. Furthermore, she was irritable and somewhat withdrawn from activities with her friends, suggesting that she might have been fearful about the possible occurrence of other future tragedies. In these ways, disabling grief was part of the diagnosis of PTSD, due to her mother's reports that Susan was irritable, withdrawn, and less interested in engaging with her friends.

Treatment

Play therapy was the ideal way for Susan to express some of her worries. In the first session, she drew a photo of a Girl Scout who was surrounded by lots of markings; in the second session, she drew her Girl Scout troop with a similar whirlwind around it. These drawings suggested her feelings of anxiety and her need to express it, as did her repeated request to play *Battleship* in which "bombs" drop on several ships with the goal of sinking them. I did not interpret Susan's drawings to her because I thought that this would frighten her, but I did make comments directed symbolically toward the theme of the game such as, "This is very scary; you never know when a bomb will drop." After a few weeks of this play, I mentioned that the bomb might kill some of the people on the ship. Susan refused to consider this possibility, saying that the people could swim to an island; she wanted to deny that death could occur randomly. Readers can find more examples in the original case presentation, but it was clear that this 9-year-old girl, who was functioning well until the tragic death of her close friend, improved significantly after seven therapy sessions in which her grief was expressed symbolically through drawings and play. She was able to receive enough relief to be symptom-free and resume her previous high level of functioning.

Approximately 9 months after therapy terminated, Susan returned for two sessions due to serious lapses in her school performance. Susan's class had been reading and discussing a book in which a boy dies, and some of her classmates spontaneously recalled their friend's tragic death. It seemed quite evident that this reminder of her close friend had contributed to the current deterioration in Susan's school performance. I was aware that many of Susan's feelings about the traumatic death had never been verbalized directly and predicted that she would probably need to engage in further therapy at a future date. This proved to be true and illustrates the concept of titrating the therapy according to an individual's needs and changing ability to cope with the stress of discussing a traumatic death.

Depression after a father's suicide (John, age 16)

This case is a compilation of several examples I know about through my readings and work as a supervisor/consultant. John was referred to a social worker in a private practice by his school counselor, who was concerned about the serious drop in his grades and his seemingly depressed mood in class. John's teachers had reported that John was looking out the window and not participating in class discussions; this behavior was a big change from earlier in the year. The school was aware that John's father, who had recently been discharged from the Army, had died by suicide 2 months before the referral. The family had been referred to grief counselors at a local hospice, but John had refused to participate in the teen grief group.

When the social worker heard these facts about John's background and his resistance to join the group, he deliberated about how to engage John in individual therapy. He decided to "make a deal" with John to give him some control over the contact, in contrast to the death of his father, a situation in which he had been helpless. When the social worker greeted John for the first time, he told him that he knew about his father's tragic death. The social worker said that it was up to John to decide if he wanted to talk about his father or not, but that if he would agree to come just three times, he could then decide whether to continue. What could be John's motivation to accept this deal? The social worker emphasized in the first meeting that John's mother was very worried about him, and of course John wouldn't want to cause her any more heartbreak. This proved to be a convincing approach, so they shook on the deal for three individual therapy sessions.

Disabling factors

John had stopped functioning in school, and everyone around him commented that he seemed depressed. As the social worker got to know John, he learned that the boy was not sleeping well, that he had lost quite a bit of weight, and that he had lost interest in his usual activities of fishing and playing basketball. He was also drinking liberally from the stash of alcohol that his father had stored in the basement. John shared that he felt guilty about his father's death, saying that he should have known that his dad was not functioning well and should have somehow done something to prevent the death. This reaction is common among suicide survivors. John also admitted that he had not wanted to attend the bereavement group because he was embarrassed to admit to the nature of his father's death. The stigma associated with a suicidal death, often causing strong feelings of shame and attempts to remain isolated and removed from others, is based in the belief that others cannot understand their profound feelings of rejection, anger, and blame (Kaslow, Samples, Rhodes, & Gantt, 2011). In addition, according to Cerel and Aldrich, "Adolescents who had experienced a suicidal death by a family member were 2.5 times more likely to report suicidal ideation and 6.5 times more likely to have a history of their own suicide attempts in the past year" (2011, p. 85). They are also more likely to participate in risky behavior and to become involved in alcohol and drug use. It became clear that engaging John before his problems grew worse could serve an important preventive purpose. The disabling factors here included the boy's avoidance of contact with others, his use of alcohol, his poor school performance, and the possibility that his guilt over his father's death might precipitate his own suicidal ideation or attempts.

Treatment

The social worker saw his role as that of a supportive advisor, with the goal of establishing a trusting relationship with John so that he could begin to grieve the loss of his father. He began by suggesting that John tell him all the special things he liked about his father and also, if he wanted, to share any of his negative memories. The social worker then said if he didn't want to talk that was fine. John seemed to waver between feeling proud of his dad for serving in the military and feeling angry and resentful about it because it meant that his dad wasn't around to coach his basketball games or do "guy stuff" together. He was aware that his dad was upset because he hadn't received a job offer he wanted and that his dad was drinking a great deal when he was home alone. John thought that he should have somehow stopped his dad from drinking and made his dad feel better. The social worker validated these feelings, but he gently pointed out that kids simply don't have the power to control an adult's destructive behavior.

The social worker asked John if he would like to connect with another young person in a military family whose father had died by suicide and John eagerly agreed. He contacted the Tragedy Assistance Program for Survivors (TAPS) and arranged for a peer mentor for John. This nationwide program offers contact with trained peer counselors who themselves are suicide survivors, a web site, chat rooms, and a 2-day Good Grief Camp for children and adolescents for any military family whose loved one has died (Harrington-LaMorie & Ruocco, 2011). Once John was connected with his peer mentor, his social worker felt confident that John's bereavement needs would be met by talking with other survivors who had endured similar feelings of disabling grief after the suicide of a family member, that he would be able to reconnect with friends and activities, and that he would pledge to stop drinking.

Disabling grief after a husband's sudden death
(Louise, age 58, a composite case)

Louise was a successful business manager and had been married to Tom, an ambitious lawyer, for 30 years. The couple had two adult children and four grandchildren. The marriage had its difficulties but was energized through expensive vacations and family gatherings on holidays and birthdays. Louise loved her job and planned to continue working until she was 65. Tom was also ambitious, even bringing work home on weekends. He left the house at 7 a.m. and returned around 6 p.m. after a difficult commute.

One morning when she had just arrived at work, Louise received a telephone call from the local hospital stating that Tom had been in a car accident, had had a heart attack, and now was in intensive care. By the time Louise arrived at the hospital, Tom had stopped breathing and been declared dead. Louise screamed in disbelief and spent several minutes stroking Tom's face and talking to him; she then found herself filling out paperwork and beginning burial arrangements. Louise kept saying, "It's not supposed to be like this; we had plans for the future; I can't imagine living by myself."

Louise did not want a funeral or memorial service; their friends and coworkers were told that they could contribute to a charity of their choice in Tom's honor. His body was cremated and Louise placed the urn on a dresser in her bedroom. Louise's adult children, both of whom lived out of town with their families, came to visit and console her. She seemed detached and in a world of her own, but convinced them that she was fine and that she would be returning to work soon. After the week of family bereavement leave permitted by her company, Louise's family returned to their homes, with a plan in place to call Louise several times a week.

Louise returned to work, but her coworkers noticed that she did not seem like herself. She appeared tired and sometimes seemed to have problems concentrating. She was often late and did not engage in any small talk during lunch hour, unlike her typical behavior prior to Tom's death. She also ate little lunch and after 3 months began to look thin and frail. She often wore the same outfit and did not seem to care about her appearance as she had done previously. A coworker who actively participated with Louise in a monthly book club was surprised when Louise said that she had lost interest in reading and wasn't going to attend anymore. The co-worker called Louise's daughter and expressed concern about her mother's behavior changes. When her daughter hastily arranged a visit after not seeing her mother for about a month, she was surprised to find the house in disarray and the refrigerator almost empty. Louise's daughter was concerned enough to make an appointment with her mother's family physician. The doctor noticed the change in Louise's appearance and her lack of responsiveness and arranged a referral to a bereavement specialist. Louise reluctantly agreed to go, mainly because of her daughter's insistence.

Disabling factors

It was evident to people who knew Louise that she was not functioning in the competent and energetic manner typical of her work style. She was going through the motions, but seemed to be doing so in a robotic manner. She was not eating and had lost significant weight. She was paying little attention to her physical appearance and her home and had stopped participating in activities that she previously enjoyed. These elements together suggested Louise's functioning had become seriously impaired, clearly indicating a disabling grief response.

Treatment

In their first meeting, the psychologist talked with both Louise and her daughter, reviewing Louise's family background while also looking for behavioral indications that would constitute a diagnosis of depression or PTSD. Many of Louise's symptoms were consistent with those of a major depressive disorder (MDD) as far as she was exhibiting a depressed mood most of the day, a diminished interest in activities most of the time, weight loss, insomnia, fatigue, and loss of energy. According to the *DSM-5* (APA, 2013), these five symptoms (out of a total of nine possibilities), combined with the requirement that they cause significant distress and are not attributable to other factors, convinced the psychologist that the diagnosis of MDD was the most appropriate in Louise's case. He recommended that Louise receive a low dose of medication together with weekly therapy to monitor and improve her emotional and physical well-being. Louise, in part due to her daughter's insistence, agreed and began a regimen of therapy that helped restore her functioning within a few months.

TREATMENT CONSIDERATIONS

The death of a close friend, relative, or family member inevitably results in distress and pain over the loss. This chapter considered the nature of this reaction relative to the degree of distress and to the factors that make the particular grief response disabling. It is worth noting that some impaired functioning is almost inevitable after any death due to the emotional toll of the grief process, which can consume and overwhelm an individual. Although most individuals endure their grief and recover on their own, a careful assessment can identify those who are still struggling after a period of several months and who will benefit from treatment.

Everyone who is bereaved has a distinctive psychosocial history, and this previous background plays a major role in the individual's response to a loss. It is only logical that someone who has experienced other deaths and who has few supports will feel a new loss more intensely than someone who has not had previous losses and who has a solid, supportive network. The specifics of the type of death (sudden or traumatic versus gradual or anticipated) also affect the reactions of survivors. One tool that summarizes and names these different contributing factors is the Tripartite Assessment, which takes into consideration (a) the individual; (b) the circumstances related to the death; and (c) the context of family, social, religious, and cultural considerations (Webb, 1993; 2002; 2010). The case examples in this chapter illustrate how the person's age and degree of family support combine to affect his or her response to a death.

Practitioners and educators will benefit from considering the three interweaving factors from the Tripartite Assessment in their efforts to understand the nature and impact of any disabling grief response. When the degree of disability interferes with the ability of the mourner to carry on with his or her life after several months, it is appropriate to recommend some form of therapeutic support, depending on the age of the survivor and the nature of the bereavement situation. Crenshaw (2008) and Worden (1991) emphasize the importance of distinguishing between individuals who are exhibiting serious problems and those who are simply struggling with their grief responses. The assessment and evaluation of the bereaved individual can result in the recommendation for either bereavement support and counseling or grief therapy (Worden, 1991). In the three cases presented here, Susan responded to short-term play therapy, John benefited from the support of other teen survivors in a group for adolescents bereaved by suicide, and Louise needed in-depth psychotherapy in addition to medication.

Individuals who are experiencing disabling grief can be helped. The first step in providing this help involves conveying the message that such disabling responses are normal and adaptive reactions to loss and that different forms of helpful treatment are available to reduce the painful and disturbing feelings that occur and persist.

Nancy Boyd Webb, DSW, LICSW, RPT-S, is a professor emerita, an author/editor, keynote speaker, and workshop presenter. Her areas of expertise include traumatic bereavement, play therapy, and vicarious traumatization. Her keynote presentations and workshops focus on these topics as they affect children, adolescents, and their families. Webb held the endowed James R. Dumpson Chair in Child Welfare Studies at Fordham University, where she taught in the Clinical Practice area for 30 years and was named University Distinguished Professor. In 1985 she founded Fordham's Post-Master's Certificate Program in Child and Adolescent Therapy, which continued for 22 years until her retirement. Smith College honored Dr. Webb with its prestigious Day/Garrett award in 2010. In addition to teaching, writing, supervising practitioners, and consulting with schools and agencies, Dr. Webb participates in several interdisciplinary professional organizations. Her bestselling books are considered essential references for university clinical courses and for agencies and practitioners.

REFERENCES

American Psychiatric Association. (2013). *Diagnostic and statistical manual of mental disorders* (5th ed.). Washington, DC: American Psychiatric Association.

Bonanno, G. A., Wortman, C. B., Lehman, D. R., Tweed, R. G., Haring, M, Sonnega, J., & Nesse, R. M. (2002). Resilience to loss and chronic grief: A prospective study from preloss to 18-months postloss. *Journal of Personality and Social Psychology*, 83, 1150-1164.

Cerel, J. & Aldrich, R. S. (2011). The impact of suicide on children and adolescents. In J. R. Jordan & J. L. McIntosh (Eds.), *Grief after suicide. Understanding the consequences and caring for the survivors*, pp. 81-92. New York, NY: Routledge.

Crenshaw, D. A. (2008). Grief therapy with children and adolescents: An overview. In K. J. Doka & A. S. Tucci (Eds.), *Living with grief: Children and adolescents* (pp. 217-231). Washington, DC: Hospice Foundation of America.

Harrington-LaMorie, J., & Ruocco, K. (2011). The Tragedy Assistance Program for Survivors (TAPS). In J. R. Jordan & J. L. McIntosh (Eds.), *Grief after suicide: Understanding the consequences and caring for the survivors*, pp. 403-411. New York, NY: Routledge.

Helping Hand (December 23, 2012). New targeted therapy helps overcome disabling grief. (NIMH—13). Medford, NJ: Helping Hand Grief Support.

Jordan, A. H. & Litz, B. T. (2014). Prolonged grief disorder: Diagnostic, assessment, and treatment considerations. *Professional psychology: Research and practice*, 45:3, 180-187.

Kaslow, N. J., Samples, T. C., Rhodes, M., & Gantt, S. (2011). A family-oriented and culturally sensitive postvention approach with suicide survivors. In J. R. Jordan & J. L McIntosh (Eds.), *Grief after suicide: Understanding the consequences and caring for the survivors.* New York, NY: Routledge.

Prigerson, H. G., Horowitz, M. J., Jacobs, S. C., Parkes, C. M., Aslan, M., Goodkin, K., Raphael, B., & Maciejewski, P. K. (2009). Prolonged grief disorder: Psychometric validation of criteria proposed for DSM-V and ICD-11. *PLoS Medicine*, 6, e1000121. doi:10.1371/journal.pmed.1000121

Webb, N. B. (Ed.). (1993). *Helping bereaved children. A handbook for practitioners.* New York, NY: Guilford Press.

Webb, N. B. (Ed.). (2002). *Helping bereaved children. A handbook for practitioners,* 2nd ed. New York, NY: Guilford Press.

Webb, N. B. (Ed.). (2010). *Helping bereaved children. A handbook for practitioners,* 3rd ed., New York, NY: Guilford Press.

Worden, J. W. (1991). *Grief counseling and grief therapy: A handbook for the mental health practitioner* (2nd ed.). New York, NY: Springer.

CHAPTER 4

Complicated Grief:
A Cross-Cultural Perspective

Paul C. Rosenblatt

Mental health professionals and grief scholars who write about complicated grief are not in full accord about what it is (Harvey, 2014; Stroebe & Schut, 2005-2006; Stroebe, Schut, & van den Bout, 2013). For the sake of grounding this chapter, complicated grief is defined as having several different expressions. The one that has received the most attention in the literature consists of severe grief reactions extended out beyond 6 months from the death. These reactions include frequent strong expressions of sadness and grief, ongoing preoccupation with the deceased, ongoing anger and bitterness about the death, ongoing estrangement from others as a consequence of psychological or psychosocial processes connected to the death, and significant impairment in occupational functioning. Alternatively, grief can be considered complicated if a major loss seems to have little or no impact, what could be called absent, muted, or delayed grief. Thus, for purposes of this chapter, grief becomes complicated when it goes on strongly for too long, when it disrupts relationships and work life, or when it is absent or seems to be too little.

COMPLICATED GRIEF IS A CONCEPT FROM
A PARTICULAR CULTURE

The concepts and standards in psychiatry, psychology, social work, and related mental health fields in Western culture of what is healthy and what is not are thoroughly entangled in the biases, values, and beliefs of Western culture (Caplan, 1985; Charmaz & Milligan, 2006; Fabrega, 1987; Rosenblatt, 2012). Complicated grief (including the related concepts of prolonged grief disorder and persistent complex bereavement disorder) is no different. It comes from, fits, and serves a particular culture. It is a cultural concept using the metaphor of illness borrowed from Western cultural concepts of physical illness. One sign that complicated grief is a metaphor or conceptual model is that there is no research showing a clear biological basis to complicated grief. Complicated grief does not arise from the invasion of bacteria or a virus. It does not arise from malfunction of cells or organs. It does not arise from physical damage to the body. Complicated grief is a cultural concept that draws on concepts of physical illness for meaning and importance. Metaphoric borrowing is a legitimate and often useful path to understanding things, but it is very risky to reify metaphors and treat them as though they have a concrete reality. So, it is important to consider the metaphoric nature of the concept of complicated grief and the cultural context in which it was developed. Because the concept of complicated grief comes from a particular culture, professionals must use caution in applying it to people of diverse cultures. To do otherwise is to be disrespectful to people from diverse cultures, to be closed to understanding the realities of those people, and to say that if they do not fit the realities of a particular culture that is not their own there is something wrong with them.

The major writings by the therapists and researchers who have defined complicated grief and made the case for it being a mental health problem do not say explicitly, as far as I know, that their concept applies to people of all cultures. In fact, there is mention in some of those writings of the need for attention to cultural differences, particularly cultural differences in the somatization of grief, the ways in which the bodies of people in diverse cultures diversely express and symbolize their feelings of loss. But overall, in the major writings, few words are devoted to culture. The language of the defining works dealing with complicated grief is usually in a generalizing, "we-are-writing-about-humanity" form, a language form that is standard in the mental health field. It is a form that is often criticized as misleading, as a rhetorical move that is intended to persuade rather than language founded on extensive research on the diversity of the species. But the language form is engrained in psychology and other mental health fields. At the very least, researchers and clinicians should be wary of generalizing language that seems to say that all humans are the same, especially because such language means that cultural differences might have been slighted or ignored.

IDEAS FROM OTHER CULTURES ABOUT PROBLEMATIC GRIEVING

The idea that some people who are grieving are in trouble makes sense in many cultures. But to define what the trouble is on the basis of the standards of a particular culture is quite an overextension. In fact, in many cultures, what would be seen in the mental health literature from North America and Western Europe as complicated grief is accepted, makes sense, and is not seen as something for intervention. For example, Wikan (1988) wrote about how a mother in Cairo, Egypt, grieved the death of her child intensely for 7 years, acting depressed, withdrawn, inactive, almost mute, and seemingly self-absorbed. Her reaction was seen among her friends, family, and neighbors as appropriate, not as pathological but as sane, making perfect sense culturally.

There are also many examples in the anthropological literature of cultures where there are concerns about people who grieve too much, too little, or behave in some other way that does not fit what is common and expected in the culture. But none of these cultures has the concept of complicated grief or use medical or psychotherapeutic language to understand and treat such grieving. One thing this implies is that had people from one of these other cultures, not the experts who gave us the concept of complicated grief, set the standards, we might have an extremely different notion of when grief is problematic.

Culturally problematic loss issues in two Buddhist cultures

The following examples from Buddhist cultures can help make the case against the current culture-bound thinking about complicated grief and against applying that culture-bound thinking to people of diverse cultures.

Hyolmo grieving

The Hyolmo, a Buddhist people who are ethnically Tibetan, are concentrated in the Hyolmo Valley of Nepal. According to Robert Desjarlais (2016), an anthropologist who studied the Hyolmo beginning in the late 1980s, problematic Hyolmo grieving, grieving that would call for help from others, most often is about what the grieving of the living does to the person who has died. Close family members and friends of a person who has died will certainly cry, but the Hyolmo would be concerned about someone grieving too intensely and openly in the first 49 days after a death. In Hyolmo Buddhist thought, the consciousness of the deceased survives after death and remains in the vicinity where the death occurred for up to 49 days. During that time the consciousness needs help to end its attachments to the living. If the living grieve too much, it becomes difficult for the consciousness of the deceased to move onward toward the next rebirth or to the Pure Land, a region of respite from the cycle of birth and death. Further, if a survivor is grieving too much, there is risk that the consciousness of the deceased could do harm to that survivor, perhaps even claiming the survivor's life. The Hyolmo offer a view that challenges the standard definition of complicated grief in that their greatest concern about grief that deviates from cultural standards is in the first 7 weeks following a death. They are not concerned about the mental health of someone who grieves too much but about the potential problems the consciousness of the deceased will have and the possible harm that consciousness may cause the living if the living grieve improperly.

Cambodian refugee grieving

Hinton and colleagues (2013) studied Cambodian refugees, all of whom were Buddhists and living in the Boston area. These Cambodian refugees were all bereaved because of deaths during the Cambodian genocide that wiped out 25% of the people of Cambodia in the late 1970s. The deaths during the genocide were quintessentially "bad deaths" in Cambodian Buddhist cultural views: deaths as the result of violence or starvation and deaths when a person was not at peace while dying and among loving family members. Worse yet, the Cambodians who lost loved ones during the genocide were not able to carry out the proper Buddhist funeral ceremonies for their deceased relatives.

In contrast to the complicated grief concept, in Cambodian thought, when a person dies a "bad death" or when a person does not receive the proper funeral ceremonies, "the dead may not move on to the next spiritual level to become spiritual helpers but instead may roam the earth in a wretched state and pose a danger to the living" (Hinton et al., 2013, p. 429). So, the long-term, ongoing, intense grief of the Cambodian refugees was not, in Cambodian refugee thinking, a matter of psychological complications for the living but of spiritual problems for the deceased because of how the death occurred and because the proper death rituals were not carried out. The concerns seen by Hinton and colleagues do not easily fit into psychological concepts about emotional dysfunction; they are about spiritual problems.

Concerns about the spiritual status of their loved ones continue to nag at the Cambodians because they still have obligations to the dead and because the dead are still a spiritual presence and potentially a danger to the living.

Many of the grieving Cambodian refugees had dreams of the dead. These dreams were seen by the Cambodians as a sign that the deceased were not at peace, were still nearby, and were potentially dangerous. The dreams were experienced by the refugees as real interactions with the spirit of the deceased person. Thus, the Cambodian refugees not only felt grief for their deceased loved ones, but also felt that the spirits of the loved ones were in trouble, communicating, and even potentially posing a threat.

Hinton and colleagues did not say that the idea of complicated grief should be abandoned. Instead, they advocated for views of complicated grief with culturally-specific components. For instance, how complicated grief was defined for Cambodian refugees in the study would overlap with the standard definitions of complicated grief, but would also have culture-specific elements added and, perhaps, some of the components of the standard definition of complicated grief removed because they do not fit Cambodian culture. In terms of intervention and support, I can appreciate that point of view, though I would also say that the Cambodian refugees might not need standard treatments for complicated grief but help carrying out rituals that would address the ongoing spiritual problems created by the "bad deaths" and the failure to carry out proper rituals soon after those deaths.

Hinton and his colleagues also wrote about culturally standard ways of expressing sadness and concerns about the dead (dizziness, for example, among Cambodian refugees) that are outside of the standard lists of symptoms in complicated grief. Culturally sensitive work with the bereaved, including work within a complicated grief framework, needs to become more attuned to cultural differences in how people grieve.

A further challenging issue is that many, if not all, of the Cambodian refugees studied by Hinton and colleagues had their own traumatic experiences to deal with. They could be in need of help in dealing with their own personal trauma as well as addressing their grieving; we should not assume that effective trauma treatment can be the same across cultures.

What the two Buddhist examples suggest about complicated grief

The two Buddhist examples challenge the cultural universality of the concept of complicated grief and suggest that one needs to be very cautious in extending the concept of complicated grief to people of diverse cultures. These people may have their own ideas of what constitutes normal grief and what constitutes grief that is concerning. Within these cultures may be their own approaches to dealing with grief that is concerning, and those approaches may not resemble at all what a mental health professional who is knowledgeable about complicated grief would use.

While these issues are conceptual, they do impact the discussion about what standards will be applied to real people. At the county hospital near where I live, there are translators present or on call for over 200 different languages. There are staff members from dozens of cultures, and many staff members have had substantial training and experience in working with patients from cultures other than their own. In my opinion, mental health professionals should not be applying the concept of complicated grief to people of all cultures. They must respect and understand the diverse ways people grieve and the diverse meanings and experiences that underlie how they grieve.

African-American versus European-American grieving

I would even make the case that what is for the most part shared culture between groups in the United States is not necessarily shared when it comes to grieving. For instance, research has shown a degree of differences in grieving between African Americans and European Americans, with bereaved African Americans scoring higher than European Americans on measures of complicated grief (e.g., Goldsmith, Morrison, Vanderwerker, & Prigerson, 2008; Laurie & Neimeyer, 2008). Writings reporting these differences use the concept of complicated grief and a belief in the value of associated measures to suggest that African Americans are on average more likely to need grief counseling, bereavement support, and related services. But is a complicated grief framework the proper one for understanding the situation of grieving African Americans and for defining what sort of help African Americans who grieve strongly for more than a few months need?

I would not want to deny anyone who desires counseling, bereavement support, and related services such assistance. And one can certainly make the case that racism and discrimination make it more likely that there might be complicating issues for a bereaved African American (Barrett, 2009; Rosenblatt & Wallace, 2005a, 2005b). But there are other ways to understand the racial differences in complicated grief that raise questions about what needs to be done. There is a view of bereavement held by some African Americans that sees the grieving of European Americans as problematically restrained (Rosenblatt & Wallace, 2005a, pp. 153-165; Staples, 1976, p. 77). That is, some African Americans see the grief of European Americans as either too bottled up or not even present. Along with this, there is often the belief among African Americans that European-American culture does not give people room to grieve adequately. From that perspective, one can wonder whether, if African Americans had taken the lead in developing the concept of complicated grief and the measures that go with it, the concept and measures would have identified African-American grieving, which is less constrained, as the normative standard for grief. Then research would show that European Americans, rather than African Americans, are more likely to have complicated grief and need help with issues of grieving.

From another perspective, pathologizing strong grief reactions can be seen as a way to mislabel or silence strong and prolonged grieving of deaths caused by social injustice (Granek, 2014). That is, labeling strong and prolonged grief reactions as a sign of psychological difficulty could be seen as a way to silence people whose strong grief reactions are in part about loved ones, now dead, being harmed by racist oppression. In my own research (Rosenblatt & Wallace, 2005a) on African-American grief, close to half the African Americans interviewed said that racism contributed to or was the cause of their loved one's death, most often racism perceived in the medical system (for example, delayed provision of medical services or provision of poor or even harmful medical services). And many talked about how racism had been a difficulty or a source of harm in the life of the loved one whose death they grieved (Rosenblatt & Wallace, 2005b). Thus, another way to look at the stronger and more prolonged grieving of the average of African Americans is that the strong grieving might in part be a strong reaction to social conditions and perceptions of injustice connected to the death being grieved. Labeling those reactions within the context of a mental health diagnostic system and making it a pathology of emotionality seems to miss how much the larger system needs to change. From that perspective, one can make the case that those of us who work at helping grieving people might do well to put substantial energy into reducing racial tensions and enhancing social justice.

THE CULTURAL CONTEXT OF THE CONCEPT OF COMPLICATED GRIEF

I think the concept of complicated grief, a concept phrased to apply to people in general and focusing primarily on helping people not to grieve too intensely for too long, did not arise accidentally in North American and Western European culture. I think it comes from the heart of the culture. There are many aspects of that, but at this point I want to mention two that I think are particularly relevant.

North American and Western European culture is one in which employers need workers to work. Most adults need to work to keep on eating, living in a dwelling, clothing themselves, and meeting their other material needs. So, concerns about complicated grief seem connected to how the economic system works in North America and Western Europe (cf. Granek, 2014). It is no accident then that the concept of complicated grief includes impairment in occupational functioning. People are expected to do their work, no matter what has happened in their lives. In fact, people whose work is impaired by bereavement will be threatened with job loss or may actually lose their job (e.g., Rosenblatt, 2000, pp. 225-226).

Then, too, in the United States, the healthcare system is, for most people, a system influenced by insurance reimbursement. To get the help they need with what might be taken as mental health issues, people must fit the diagnostic system the insurance companies use. If they do not, insurance will not pay for their need to be met. From that perspective, the mental health professionals and researchers who created the concept of complicated grief were doing something to help many people who wanted the help of a mental health professional to address their grief issues. And since insurance companies are not in the business of treating "illnesses" that only people in certain cultures have, defining complicated grief as a universal human condition is an act of helping some bereaved people. I regret that the concept of complicated grief creates the problems it does for people from diverse cultures, but I understand how, in the United States, the concept also may help some people to receive grief support services they might desire and might otherwise not receive.

Helping culturally diverse grievers

If we do not define prolonged grief (or muted or absent grief) as illness but we are asked for help by someone from a diverse culture who seems to be grieving too long, too intensely, or too little, what can we do? There is no simple answer to the question. But here are some suggestions for what could be done that might be culturally respectful.

Provide services outside the insurance system

Determining when grief becomes complicated is clearly based on a wide range of considerations, many of which do not fall into diagnostic "codes." Sometimes it may be most helpful to provide help outside of the insurance system for people from diverse cultures. That is not as challenging as it may seem, since in many areas grief support services are available through voluntary and community agencies.

If services are provided within the insurance system, be exquisitely sensitive to cultural issues and what people say they feel, want, and need. Do not assume that an intervention that might work with some people who are said to have complicated grief works with everyone or is even tolerable and relevant to everyone.

Do not pathologize

The language of complicated grief, to the extent that it implies pathology, may put up an enormous wall with people from some cultures, drive them away, and make them distrustful. It also may make us would-be helpers seem insensitive in trying to deal with them. Instead of pathologizing with a diagnosis that says that something is wrong with an individual, we can try to help the person with what they want help with, in the ways they want help. And that includes respecting the language they use in talking about what they feel, want, and need, and understanding them in terms of their own cultural beliefs, practices, and ways of expressing emotion. What they need might not be empathic listening or wise and knowledgeable advice but help making sacrifices, help communicating with spirits of the deceased, appreciation for why grieving so long is meaningful and important, help gaining the forgiveness of the deceased, or something else that might be strange for those of us who are accustomed to thinking of standard grief support in a North American or Western European framework.

If you must work within a complicated grief model, focus on meaning-making as a tool that can be sensitive, if used wisely, to the cultural meaning systems of the person you are trying to help. You do not have to believe what people in need of help believe in order to help them to get to meanings that make sense to them concerning, for example, the anger of their deceased relatives who are still acting in their life.

In addition, focusing on the grief of individuals can make us quick to discount or ignore what people say about the political, economic, or environmental context of their loss. That, too, needs to be understood, respected, validated, and appreciated. In such a situation, a first and key step in providing grief support is to understand and respect the client's viewpoint about the conditions underlying his or her loss, even if the client's viewpoint does not fit with what is comfortable or socially acceptable for the mental health professional. In doing so, the mental health professional, by understanding the cultural context and the client's perception of the loss, can perhaps help to mitigate the inherent distrust of clients who have experienced discrimination, prejudice, and oppression.

Paul C. Rosenblatt, PhD in Psychology, is professor emeritus of Family Social Science at the University of Minnesota. He has carried out ethnographic fieldwork in Mexico and Indonesia, and has written in collaboration with natives of Korea, South Africa, and China about family life in those countries. Rosenblatt is co-author (with R. Patricia Walsh and Douglas A. Jackson) of Grief and Mourning in Cross-Cultural Perspective. *Within the US some of his research has dealt with African-American families in the context of ongoing oppression in the larger society. His publications related to that research include* African American Grief *(with Beverly R. Wallace) and* The Impact of Racism on African-American Families. *Rosenblatt has also studied intercultural and interracial couples; among his publications in that area is* Multiracial Couples *(with Terri A. Karis and Richard Powell).*

REFERENCES

Barrett, R. (2009). Sociocultural considerations: African Americans, grief, and loss. In K. J. Doka & A. S. Tucci (Eds.), *Living with grief: Diversity and end-of-life care* (pp. 79-91), Washington, DC: Hospice Foundation of America.

Caplan, P. J. (1985). *They say you're crazy: How the world's most powerful psychiatrists decide who's normal*. Reading, MA: Addison-Wesley.

Charmaz, K., & Milligan, M. J. (2006). Grief. In J. E. Stets & J. H. Turner (Eds.), *Handbook of the sociology of emotion* (pp. 516-543). New York, NY: Springer.

Desjarlais, R. (2016). *Subject to death: Loss in a Buddhist world*. Chicago, IL: University of Chicago Press.

Fabrega, H., Jr. (1987). Psychiatric diagnosis: A cultural perspective. *Journal of Nervous and Mental Disease, 175*, 383-394.

Goldsmith, B., Morrison, R. S., Vanderwerker, L. C., & Prigerson, H. G. (2008*)*. Elevated rates of prolonged grief disorder in African Americans. *Death Studies, 32*, 352-365.

Granek, L. (2014). Mourning sickness: The politicizations of grief. *Review of General Psychology, 18*(2), 61-68.

Harvey, J. H. (2014). Concluding thoughts. In E. D. Miller (Ed.), *Stories of complicated grief: A critical anthology* (pp. 341-347). Washington, DC: National Association of Social Workers Press.

Hinton, D. E., Peou, S., Joshi, S., Nickerson, A., & Simon, N. M. (2013). Normal grief and complicated bereavement among traumatized Cambodian refugees: Cultural context and the central role of dreams of the dead. *Culture, Medicine, and Psychiatry, 37*, 427-464.

Laurie, A., & Neimeyer, R. A. (2008). African Americans in bereavement: Grief as a function of ethnicity. *OMEGA—Journal of Death and Dying, 57*, 173-193.

Miller, E. D. (2014). Preface. In E. D. Miller (Ed.), *Stories of complicated grief: A critical anthology* (pp. ix-xviii). Washington, DC: National Association of Social Workers Press.

Rosenblatt, P. C. (2000). *Parent grief: Narratives of loss and relationship*. New York, NY: Routledge.

Rosenblatt, P. C. (2012). The concept of complicated grief: Lessons from other cultures. In H. Schut, P. Boelen, J. van den Bout, & M. Stroebe (Eds.), *Complicated grief: Scientific foundations for health professionals* (pp. 27-39). New York, NY: Routledge.

Rosenblatt, P. C., & Wallace, B. R. (2005a). *African American grief.* New York, NY: Routledge.

Rosenblatt, P. C., & Wallace, B. R. (2005b). Narratives of grieving African-Americans about racism in the lives of deceased family members. *Death Studies, 29,* 217-235.

Staples, R. (1976). *Introduction to Black sociology.* New York, NY: McGraw Hill.

Stroebe, M., & Schut, H. (2005-2006). Complicated grief: A conceptual analysis of the field. *OMEGA—Journal of Death and Dying, 52,* 53-70.

Stroebe, M., Schut, H., & van den Bout, J. (2013). Introduction: Outline of goals and scope of the book. In M. Stroebe, H. Schut, & J. van den Bout (Eds.), *Complicated grief: Scientific foundations for health care professionals* (pp. 3-9). New York, NY: Routledge.

Wikan, U. (1988). Bereavement and loss in two Muslim communities: Egypt and Bali compared. *Social Science and Medicine, 27,* 451-460.

CHAPTER 5

Is Grief Complicated?
The Dangers of a Label

Donna L. Schuurman

Grief is neither a problem to be solved nor a disease to be cured.
Stuart Farber, MD

The issues related to defining the characteristics, course, and symptoms of normal grief, and by extension, abnormal grief, have been widely debated over the past several decades and remain subjects of considerable controversy. Scholars from the fields of psychology and psychiatry, as well as thanatology, sociology, traumatology, neurobiology, and pharmacology (among others), variously weigh in to the discussions of what might be considered outside of the range of normal human response to loss and therefore, and of no small importance, how to best respond to and support those who are grieving.

In 1917, Freud stated in his essay *Mourning and Melancholia* that "although mourning involves grave departures from the normal attitude to life, it never occurs to us to regard it as a pathological condition and to refer it to medical treatment" (p. 252). Fast forward to 2001, when the term traumatic grief was commonly used, as in this description of Traumatic Grief Treatment: "The treatment, considered a medical intervention, is aimed at healing the disturbance in a natural restorative process, facilitating any remaining grief, and reestablishing psychosocial functioning" (Shear, Zuckoff, & Frank, 2001). While it is beyond the scope of this chapter to comprehensively explore the historical underpinnings of this discussion, Granek (2010) provides a compelling look at how "grief has been constructed as a pathological condition necessitating psychological intervention in order for people to heal as quickly as possible" (p. 48).

Over the years, the proposed labels for grief that seems to be more intense or last longer than what is considered normal have numbered in the dozens; some of the most favored have included pathological grief, traumatic grief, prolonged grief, and complicated grief. These terms share some commonalities, but also significant differences, related largely to the intensity and/or duration of symptoms. Advocates for conceptualizing grief as a pathology or disorder, as well as those opposed, agree in theory that the experience of grief is both complex and complicated. The questions that widen the gap of disagreement are both theoretical and clinical. Upon what premises, assumptions, and beliefs might we label grief as pathology? Who decides what specific symptoms or behaviors constitute such a disorder? And what are the potential rewards and risks of labeling reactions to a death as a form of "complicated grief" requiring professional intervention?

The answers to these questions have broad and serious implications for grieving individuals and communities, as well as political, financial, and social consequences. As medical philosopher Lawrie Reznek (1987) noted in *The Nature of Disease*, "Concepts carry consequences—classifying things one way rather than another has important implications for the way we behave toward such things" (p. 1). While other researchers and clinicians address the potential rewards of a grief-related mental disorder, the focus here will be on the risks and downsides of doing so.

To be clear, arguments against conceptualizing grief as a mental disorder do not mean all grievers will be fine without support or intervention or that quality professional help is never warranted. Pre-existing issues, whether personal, like drug addiction or clinical depression, or situational, like coping with financial or relational problems, may be heightened after someone experiences the death of a family member or friend. Parents often report social isolation after the death of their child; widows and widowers frequently experience depression and loss of energy or appetite, among a host of other emotions and what some refer to as "symptoms." Previously-held spiritual beliefs may be questioned, unaddressed issues revealed, and the sheer "before and after"-ness of grieving a person's death can shake one to the core. Despite the oft-stated "time heals all wounds," we know that time alone does not heal psychological, spiritual, and emotional wounds any more than the passage of time heals physical wounds.

There is a difference, however, between acknowledging that grief is complicated and labeling it a mental disorder necessitating treatment.

The controversy grew with the nearing of the publication in 2013 of the first full update in nearly 20 years of the American Psychiatric Association's *Diagnostic and Statistical Manual of Mental Disorders* (5th ed.; *DSM-5*; 2013). Sometimes referred to as the "bible of psychiatry," the *DSM* is owned, controlled, and sold by one entity, the American Psychiatric Association (APA). Its use as a diagnostic tool and for insurance-approved reimbursement is largely restricted to usage in the U.S. healthcare system and not without criticism. In addition to the monopoly of ownership and income rights, the *DSM* is frequently criticized for its lack of validity – "a quality of measurement indicating the degree to which the measure reflects the underlying construct, that is, whether it measures what it purports to measure" (validity, n.d.). In fact, when the *DSM-5* was published in 2013, the then director of the National Institute of Mental Health (NIMH), Thomas Insel, stated that "while the *DSM* has been described as a 'Bible' for the field, it is, at best, a dictionary, creating a set of labels and defining each…The weakness is its lack of validity" (Insel, 2013).

The *DSM-5* included two much-debated changes related to grief. The first was the removal of the "bereavement exclusion" under the category of major depressive disorder (MDD) (APA, 2013). The previous guidelines in the *DSM-IV* had advised clinicians not to diagnose an individual with MDD within 2 months of the death of a loved one because the symptoms of MDD would be considered normal for that period of time following a death (APA, 1980). Proponents for removing bereavement as an exclusion argued, successfully, that bereavement was the only life event stressor specifically excluded from a diagnosis of major depression and could therefore deny individuals from receiving appropriate treatment. Opponents, including the recommendation of a workgroup within the Association for Death Education and Counseling, concluded that "…the negative impact of dropping the bereavement exclusionary criteria outweigh the benefits" (Balk, Noppe, Sandler, & Werth, 2010). Among their numerous concerns was the risk of premature antidepressant medication being prescribed to bereaved individuals as soon as 2 weeks after the death of a loved one.

The second change in the *DSM-5* was the rejection of a grief-related mental disorder (complicated grief or prolonged grief) due to insufficient evidence for recognition as a separate diagnosis. It was instead included in Section III under the category "Conditions for Further Study" and was given the name persistent complex bereavement disorder as a compromise (APA, 2013, p. 790-792). Despite this rejection, after years of study and careful analysis, the terms complicated grief and prolonged grief have infiltrated the language of mental health and grief counseling, elevated by use in peer-reviewed and professional publications, such that it has become a thing even without the official blessing of the psychiatric profession. The more widely utilized *International Classification of Diseases* (ICD), which also includes a section on mental disorders, will "likely introduce a diagnosis to recognize prolonged grief" in its next publication (Bryant, 2014, p. 21). According to the World Health Organization, about 70% of the world's health expenditures (roughly $3.5 billion in the United States annually) are allocated using the *ICD*, which many believe will ultimately supplant the *DSM* (2015).

Regardless of the ultimate outcome, here are some of the arguments against labeling grief as a mental disorder.

THE RISK OF PATHOLOGIZING A NORMAL, COMMON, INEVITABLE LIFE EVENT

Death is a universal life experience, and in death's wake it is normal, natural, as well as healthy, to grieve. We must ask ourselves who decides what is normal and what is not? Ask the bereaved mother of a deceased 18-month-old, and you will likely find a different answer than that from a large number of professionals, many of whom were not required in their master's or doctoral level training to take even a single course on grief and loss, even if it had been available at their college or university.

No one is suggesting we withhold quality intervention from bereaved individuals who are experiencing major impairment, but "there is the risk of pathologizing what are essentially individual differences and diversity in human behavior," states Ben-Zeev, Young, and Corrigan (2010). "For example, different people will have different idiosyncratic patterns of coping with the loss of a loved one that will undoubtedly be influenced by their cultural background, social context, and nature of the relationship with the individual. Although these coping behaviors may be personally adaptive for the bereaved, they might be difficult for an outside observer to understand or assess. By introducing more and more diagnoses, we may narrow what is considered the range of 'healthy functioning' to the point where few, if any, people meet such strict parameters" (p. 324). Allen Francis, MD, the chair of the *DSM-IV* Task Force and former chair of the Department of Psychiatry at Duke University, has been a vocal advocate of the concern that the changes in the *DSM-5* are overpathologizing normal human experience. This concern is reflected in the title of his 2013 book, *Saving normal: An insider's revolt against out-of-control psychiatric diagnosis,* DSM-5, *big pharma, and the medicalization of ordinary life.*

THE RISKS OF CONCEPTUALIZING GRIEF IN A WESTERN-ORIENTED MEDICAL MODEL MODALITY

What is a "mental disorder" and how has its definition shifted over the years? The *DSM-IV* stated that "A mental disorder is a clinically significant behavioral or psychological syndrome or pattern that occurs in an individual and that is associated with present distress or disability or with a significantly increased risk of suffering death, pain, disability, or an important loss of freedom." It continued on to say that "an expectable or culturally approved response to a common stressor or loss, such as the death of a loved one, is not a mental disorder" (APA, 1994, xxi).

This definition begs several questions. Who and what defines a "clinically significant" disturbance? Note that what is referred to as a "syndrome or pattern" is something that "occurs in an individual." One of the problems with viewing grief as a "mental disorder" is that doing so suggests that the causes of the person's distress and "symptoms" are located *within the individual,* failing to fully recognize the complex interactions in the person's social and cultural environment. We should also question what is "expectable or culturally approved" and whether that is the standard by which we gauge whether or not someone has a "mental disorder." This definition does not allow for the reality that much of what is both "expectable" and "culturally approved" following a death may result in bereaved people experiencing additional distress and impairment in social functioning.

The Risk of Confusing a "Construct" with a "Condition"

Complicated grief and its partner terms are often described by proponents as syndromes, conditions, or entities, but they are in fact social constructs. An entity, for example, is "a disease or condition that has separate and distinct existence and objective or conceptual reality" (entity, n.d.). The construct of complicated grief or persistent complex bereavement disorder (PCBD) is socially and culturally constructed as a list of agreed-upon symptoms clustering to formulate what a narrow group of professionals decide constitutes a mental disorder. These symptoms are largely considered normal responses to the death of a loved one, and the social construct of the mental disorder refers to either the intensity or longevity (or both) of the symptoms. A full listing of the proposed criteria A through E for PCBD may be found on pages 789-792 of the *DSM-5*, but here is one example: Under category B, one must have "…at least one of the following (4) symptoms… on more days than not and to a clinically significant degree and has persisted for at least 12 months after the death in the case of bereaved adults and 6 months for bereaved children:

1. Persistent yearning/longing for the deceased. In young children, yearning may be expressed in play and behavior, including behaviors that reflect being separated from, and also reuniting with, a caregiver or other attachment figure.
2. Intense sorrow and emotional pain in response to the death.
3. Preoccupation with the deceased.
4. Preoccupation with the circumstances of the death. In children, this preoccupation with the deceased may be expressed through the themes of play and behavior and may extend to preoccupation with possible death of others close to them" (APA, 2013).

Acknowledging that there are additional qualifiers ("D: The disturbance causes clinically significant distress or impairment in social, occupational, or other important areas of functioning") and (E: "The bereavement reaction is out of proportion to or inconsistent with cultural, religious, or age-appropriate norms"), all of these constructs should be subject to serious scrutiny (APA, 2013). What and who defines "preoccupation" with the deceased, for example? At The

Dougy Center for Grieving Children and Families, we've witnessed these "symptoms" as common, normal, and healthy responses from the thousands of youth and parents we've served since 1981. These children are frequently labeled as "acting out" because they're having difficulty sitting still or paying attention in school. Often, contributing factors include being made fun of by other kids, being expected to continue "business as usual" by school personnel, and feeling different and separate from their peers. In a mainstream society that urges them to "move on" and "get over" the death of their parent, sibling, or friend, who defines whether our "cultural, religious, or age-appropriate norms" are healthy expectations?

THE RISK OF CONFUSING SOCIAL CONSTRUCTS AS VALID SCIENCE

Those who advocate for including a grief-related mental disorder in the *DSM* point out that a diagnostic category will help provide insurance coverage (at least in the United States), spark the availability of research funding, and promote better intervention protocols for the bereaved. These goals are not without conflict, however. As stated earlier, "…the weakness is its lack of validity" (Insel, 2013). Insel was widely criticized for this statement, as well as one stating that the NIMH "will be re-orienting its research away from *DSM* categories" and "developing a more precise diagnostic system," the Research Domain Criteria (RDoC) (Insel, 2013), but the validity of the symptom approach to mental disorders is a reasonable question whose answers contain serious implications.

Hogan, Worden, and Schmidt (2003-04) conducted an empirical study of the complicated grief disorder criteria that had been proposed in 1999 by a panel of experts in loss, trauma, and the formulation of diagnostic criteria for psychiatric disorders. Noting that the original criteria were developed based on work with widows and widowers, their analysis "did not support the distinctness between complicated grief and depression, or complicated grief and normal grief," and they suggested that "both further investigation into the validity of complicated grief disorder as a diagnosis and verification of the validity of the diagnostic criteria is warranted before declaring this phenomenon appropriate for inclusion in diagnostic systems" (Hogan et. al., 2003-04, p. 263). Despite these warnings and the failure of the *DSM-5* committee to endorse and include a grief-related mental disorder, the phenomenon of complicated grief pervades bereavement journals and literature, even without consistency in definition, criteria, and generalizability to populations often not included in studies.

Assessing the number of individuals who might be afflicted with this disorder is equally confusing. Note this statement from Charles Reynolds, a geriatric psychiatrist and one of the principal researchers in a NIMH-funded study of complicated grief: "While complicated grief only affects between 10% to 20% of those suffering the loss of a loved one, it most typically is a woman in her mid-to-late 70s who lost her husband" (Carpenter, 2012). Bui, Nadal-Vicens, and Simon (2012) refer to it as a "debilitating condition" estimated "to effect 6% to 25% of individuals who experience the loss of a loved one" (p. 149). A simple search of the term "complicated grief" will yield wildly conflicting estimates of the numbers of those who experience this condition.

THE RISK OF OVERDIAGNOSIS, OVERTREATMENT, AND PHARMACEUTICAL SOLUTIONS

The combination of the removal of the bereavement exclusion under major depressive disorder and the proliferation of usage of bereavement-related mental disorder language leads many to express concern about the potential for unmonitored, unwarranted, or ill-advised rushes toward pharmaceutical solutions. Many are concerned about the increased likelihood that people will be treated with antidepressants, which have numerous side effects and dubious efficacy. Consider the words of Allen Francis: The new *DSM-5* "legalizes the marketing of grief as depression" so people "who are suffering normal grief will be far more likely to be diagnosed with depression and treated with antidepressants" (APA, 2013).

As Jerome Wakefield, professor and researcher at New York University, pointed out, "Once you classify these forms of grief as disorders, the symptoms become a target for drug development" (Whorisky, 2012). Given the large number of grieving individuals, a percentage of which may have some level of impairment, this remains a potentially attractive market for pharmaceutical research and marketing.

In 2001 a study was published which is frequently referenced to support the case for the existence of a bereavement-related mental disorder. The study was funded by a pharmaceutical company and included 22 widows/widowers whose spouses had died 4 to 6 weeks before they were given an 8-week course of the antidepressant medication Wellbutrin. It was an open trial, meaning that both the researchers and the participants knew what treatment was being administered, and the study had no control group. Apparently, the small sample of bereaved spouses showed improvement, and the lead researcher disclosed research support and/or speaking honoraria from four pharmaceutical companies (Zisook, Shuster, Pedrelli, Sable, & Deacius, 2001). The combination of an extremely small sample with an open trial, no control group, and the vested interest of the funding source calls into question not only the results of the study, but also its validity, applicability, and generalizability.

THE RISKS OF CONFLICTS OF INTEREST IMPACTING MOVEMENTS AND DECISIONS

Beyond the pharmaceutical industry, it is worth asking who else may benefit from a mental disorder diagnosis. *The New York Times* reported in 2009, after the National Alliance on Mental Illness (NAMI) refused to release details of its income, that about three-quarters of its donations, nearly $23 million over the years 2006-2008, came from drug makers (Harris, 2009).

While the *DSM-5* Task Force members were restricted to receiving $10,000 maximum annual income from pharmaceutical companies during the time period during which they served on the task force, 69% of them reported financial ties to the drug industry, a 21% increase over the *DSM-IV* (Cosgrove et al., 2014), and 67% of the *DSM-5* panel that eliminated the bereavement exclusion had ties to pharmaceutical companies that make the drugs used to treat mood disorders (Cosgrove & Krimsky, 2012). It is not unreasonable, in each of these situations, to ask about issues of transparency, and whether and in what ways decision-makers may be influenced by receiving funding and support from the pharmaceutical industry.

THE RISKS OF UNINTENDED CONSEQUENCES AND CONFOUNDING SIDE EFFECTS

Other potential implications can arise. Despite HIPAA privacy laws, there are potential consequences to having a mental disorder diagnosis in one's history. According to Joanne Cacciatore, the founder of the Center for Loss and Trauma in Phoenix and a professor of social work at Arizona State University, "Once you say someone has a mental illness and bill their insurance company, that's on their record" (Townsend, 2013). Such a record could have lifelong consequences.

THE RISKS OF LOSING TRADITIONAL AND CULTURAL METHODS OF ADAPTING TO THE LOSS OF A LOVED ONE

Handing over treatment to professionals for a grief-related disorder risks undermining some of the traditional and cultural methods of adapting to the loss of a loved one. Granek (2010) points out the major influence of the German-American psychiatrist Erich Lindemann, who is known for, among other achievements, his extensive study on the effects of traumatic events after the Cocoanut Grove night club fire in Boston in 1942 that killed 492 people and injured hundreds. Lindemann stated in his 1944 publication *Symptomatology and the Management of Acute Grief* that "at first glance, acute grief would not seem to be a medical or psychiatric disorder in the strict sense of the word, but rather a normal reaction to a distressing situation. However, the understandings of reactions to traumatic experiences whether or not they represent clear cut neuroses has become of ever increasing importance to the psychiatrist" (Lindemann, p. 141). Granek continues:

> Lindemann goes as far as to claim that while it was once the case that ministers and religious institutions used to deal with the grief stricken, 'comfort alone' from these people 'does not provide adequate assistance in the patient's grief work.' It is only a psychiatrist that can be of help to the bereaved, and the use of social workers, ministers, and family members should be for the purposes of 'urge[ing] the patient to…see a psychiatrist' (p. 147). This approach of criticizing other resources for the grieving person including religious ministers, family, and friends became a recurring theme throughout the development of grief as a psychological construct (p. 59).

In 2011, Granek and writer Meghan O'Rourke conducted a survey for the online magazine *Slate.com* about people's experiences with grief (Granek & O'Rourke, 2011). Within 7 days of posting the survey, the authors received responses from more than 8,000 individuals and noted that the information "significantly challenges contemporary psychological definitions of what grief should look and feel like, and more important, how long it should last…The process of psychologizing grief has inadvertently created a kind of public culture around mourning in which grievers feel embarrassed, uncomfortable, and unsure about whether their grief is normal or not…and perhaps most important, people seemed most of all to want a community in which to grieve but often felt alone with their mourning" (Granek, 2016).

As we have moved away from prior social support systems to a conceptualization of grief as a mental disorder requiring the intervention of professionals, we would do well to consider the balance of what we are losing against potential gains. Palliative care physician Stuart Farber, from the Department of Family Medicine at the University of Washington in Seattle, shared his experience as a patient after a diagnosis of acute myelogenous leukemia (AML) in 2013, and, almost incomprehensibly, his wife Annalu's diagnosis with AML four months later:

> The fundamental lesson I have learned as a professional patient is that clinicians and patients/families inhabit two entirely different worlds. Unfortunately, the medical world is the one that holds dominion…Loss and grief have been inseparable companions during this past year. Our grief is the natural response to the many losses we have experienced. Grief is neither a problem to be solved nor a disease to be cured. It is a process to be experienced and supported that has added richness and meaning to my life I did not know possible. Once again, grief has been one of the many paradoxes that has leavened my life. As a patient, I have been amazed at the distance my providers keep from my grief, and when it is touched, how quickly they are 'bound' to 'fixing' it. Most of my clinicians are so busy protecting themselves that 'being with me' is not possible. The lack of acknowledgment and support of my grief is a profound personal and professional lesson for me (p. 799).

Stuart Farber, husband, son, father, lover of music, avid skier, palliative care physician, died at age 67 on February 27, 2015.

Donna Schuurman, EdD, FT, *is the Senior Director of Advocacy & Training/Executive Director Emeritus for The Dougy Center for Grieving*

Children & Families, where she has served since 1986. She writes and trains internationally on children's bereavement issues and authored Never the Same: Coming to Terms with the Death of a Parent. *Dr. Schuurman is a member of the International Work Group on Death, Dying, and Bereavement, and a founding board member of The National Alliance for Grieving Children. She has trained the National Transportation Safety Board and the FBI's Rapid Deployment teams, as well as medical personnel, NGO staff and caregivers following major disasters including the Oklahoma City bombing, 9/11, Japan's 1995 Kobe earthquake and 3/11 tsunami, and the Sandy Hook School shootings in Newtown, CT. She was the recipient of the Association for Death Education and Counseling's Annual Service Award (2004) and Annual Clinical Service Award (2013).*

REFERENCES

American Psychiatric Association. (1980). *Diagnostic and statistical manual of mental disorders* (3rd ed.; *DSM-III*). Washington, DC: American Psychiatric Association.

American Psychiatric Association. (1994). *Diagnostic and statistical manual of mental disorders* (4th ed.; *DSM-IV*). Washington, DC: American Psychiatric Association.

American Psychiatric Association. (2013). *Diagnostic and statistical manual of mental disorders* (5th ed.; *DSM-5*). Washington, DC: American Psychiatric Association.

American Psychiatric Association, *What is Posttraumatic Stress Disorder?* https://www.psychiatry.org/patients-families/ptsd/what-is-ptsd

Balk, D., Noppe, I., Sandler, I., & Werth, J. (2010, Nov.). Removing the exclusionary criterion about depression in cases of bereavement: Executive summary of a report to the Board of Directors, Association for Death Education and Counseling.

Ben-Zeev, D., Young, M. A., & Corrigan, P. W. (2010). DSM-V and the stigma of mental illness. *Journal of Mental Health, 19*(4), 318-327.

Bryant, R. (2014). Prolonged Grief: Where to after diagnostic and statistical manual of mental disorders (5th edition)? *Current Opinion in Psychiatry, 27*(1): 21-26.

Bui, E., Nadal-Vicens, M., & Simon, N. (2012). Pharmacological approaches to the treatment of complicated grief: Rationale and a brief review of the literature. *Dialogues in Clinical Neuroscience, 14,* 149-157.

Carpenter, M. (2012, March). Study tries treatment for grief. Post-gazette.com. Downloaded from http://www.post-gazette.com/stories/news/health/study-tries-treatment-for-grief-245436/?p

Center for Complicated Grief. https://complicated grief.columbia.edu

Cosgrove, L., Krimsky, S., Wheeler, E., Kaitz, J., Greenspan, S., & DiPentima, N. (2014). Tripartate conflicts of interest and high stakes patent extensions in the DSM-5. *Psychotherapy and Psychosomatics, 83,* 106-113.

Cosgrove, L., & Krimsky, S. (2012). A comparison of DSM-IV and DSM-5 panel members' financial associations with industry: A pernicious problem persists. *PLos Med 9*(3): e1001190. doi: 10.1371/journal.pmed.1001190

entity. (n.d.). Retrieved December 28, 2016, from https://www.merriam-webster.com/thesaurus/entity

Farber, S. (2015). Living every minute. *Journal of Pain and Symptom Management, 49*(4), 796-800.

Francis, A. (2013). *Saving normal: An insider's revolt against out-of-control psychiatric diagnosis, DSM-5, big pharma, and the medicalization of ordinary life.* New York, NY: William Morrow.

Freud, S. (1917/1963). Mourning and Melancholia. (Johan Riviere, Trans.) In *General psychology theory*. New York, NY: Collier.

Genevro, J., Marshall, T., Miller, T., & Center for the Advancement of Health. (2004). Report on bereavement and grief research. *Death Studies. Special Issue: Report on Bereavement and Grief Research by the Center for the Advancement of Health, 28,* 491-498.

Granek, L. (2016). Medicalizing grief. In D. Harris & T. Bordere (Eds.), *Handbook of Social Justice in Loss and Grief.* London, UK: Routledge.

Granek, L. & O'Rourke, M. (Spring 2011). What is grief actually like: Results of the Slate Survey on Grief. *Slate.com*: http://www.slate.com/id/2292126/

Granek, L. (2010). Grief as pathology: The evolution of grief theory in psychology from Freud to the present. *History of Psychology*, *13*(1), 46-73.

Greenberg, G. (2013). *The Book of Woe: The DSM and the unmaking of psychiatry*. New York, NY: Blue Rider Press.

Greenberg, G. (2010). *Manufacturing depression: The secret history of a modern disease*. New York, NY: Simon & Schuster, Inc.

Harris, G. (October 21, 2009). Drug makers are advocacy group's biggest donors. *The New York Times* http://www.nytimes.com/2009/10/22/22nami.html?_r=2

Hogan, N. S., Worden, J. W., & Schmidt, L. A. (2003-04). An empirical study of the proposed complicated grief disorder criteria. *OMEGA—Journal of Death and Dying*, *48*(3), 263-277.

Insel, T. (2013, April). Director's Blog: Transforming Diagnosis. Retrieved from http://www.Nimh.nih.gov.

Kaplow, J., Layne, C., Pynoos, R., Cohen, J., & Lieberman, A. (2012). DSM-V diagnostic criteria for bereavement-related disorders in children and adolescents: Developmental considerations. *Psychiatry*, *75*(3), 243-265.

Lindemann, E. (1944). Symptomatology and management of acute grief. *American Journal of Psychiatry, 101,* 141-148.

Reznek, L. (1987). *The nature of disease*. London, UK: Routledge & Kegan Paul.

Scully, S. (2013, Winter). A new treatment program for the grief that won't end. *Spectrum Magazine.*

Shear, K., Zuckoff, A., & Frank, E. (2001). The syndrome of complicated grief. *CNS Spectrums*, 339-346.

Townsend, T. (2013, May 30). Grief: changes to psychiatric manual ignite debate over grief, mental illness and faith. *St. Louis Today.* http://www.stltoday.com/news/local/metro/changes-to-psychiatric-manual-ignite-debate-over-grief

validity. (n.d.). Retrieved December 28, 2016, from http://www.yourdictionary.com/validity

Wetherell, J. L. (2012). Complicated grief therapy as a new treatment approach. *Dialogues in Clinical Neuroscience, 14*(2), 159-166.

Whitaker, R. (2011). *Anatomy of an epidemic: Magic bullets, psychiatric drugs, and the astonishing rise of mental illness in America.* New York, NY: Broadway.

Whoriskey, P. (2012, Dec. 26). Antidepressants to treat grief? Psychiatry panelists with ties to drug industry say yes. *The Washington Post.*

World Health Organization. (2015). International classification of diseases (ICD) information sheet. Retrieved December 28, 2016, from http://www.who.int/classifications/icd/factsheet/en/

Zisook, S., Shuster, S., Pedrelli, P., Sable, J., & Deacius, S. (2001). Buproprion sustained release for bereavement: Results of an open trial. *Journal of Clinical Psychiatry, 62,* 227-230.

Treating Complicated Grief

Once complications to grief are diagnosed, clinicians need to find the most appropriate treatments. Neimeyer and Burke begin by exploring some of the risk factors that might complicate grief. In their review, they note such factors as (a) the circumstances of the death, particularly a sudden violent death; (b) the background of the bereaved, history of prior mental illness, gender, and other variables, including social class; (c) the bereaved's relationship to the deceased, both the nature of the relationship as well as other factors, such as a high level of dependency; (d) their styles of coping with the loss, such as ambivalent or avoidant attachments; and (e) the broader social and institutional systems in which they are engaged. Neimeyer and Burke's work reminds us that it is essential to assess the client's vulnerability as well as strengths. They also affirm that we should not look at such factors in isolation, but should consider how these factors impair or facilitate the client's ability to find some sense of meaning in loss.

Crenshaw's chapter adds much to the discussion of treatment. First, he explores the debate on appropriate diagnostic categories for children who seem to be experiencing more complicated reactions to loss. Crenshaw notes that while there is a lack of current consensus in diagnosis, it is critical that the small percentage of children who seem to have disabling reactions to a loss be treated lest they develop mental, or even physical, illnesses. Second, Crenshaw makes a useful distinction between bereavement and trauma, noting how the intrusive imagery introduced by a traumatic loss needs to be addressed. Finally, he uses a well-developed case study, including both information on background and treatment. His treatment plan reminds us of the value of using multiple modalities, including metaphor, art, and play therapies, in working with young clients.

Rynearson's chapter builds upon Crenshaw's observation that trauma creates particular complications for grieving individuals. Rynearson's approach also reaffirms the importance of meaning-making as a critical component of treatment. To Rynearson, the essence of treatment is highly individual. When anchored in helping the client's restorative retelling, it can help to recreate a narrative of the death that offers both meaning and comfort.

Finally, Shear's chapter completes this section and offers valuable information. She reminds readers that while many people have an acute reaction to a significant loss, in most cases, they are able to integrate that loss into their lives. Yet, Shear recognizes that some have more complicated reactions, and she offers a detailed evidence-based protocol for treating complicated grief.

This section ends on a hopeful note. Even as we strive to understand the variety of ways that individuals struggle with loss, we are developing not only better diagnostic and assessments tools, but also appropriate modalities to help bereaved individuals come to terms with their grief.

CHAPTER 6

What Makes Grief Complicated? Risk Factors for Complicated Bereavement

Robert A. Neimeyer and Laurie A. Burke

MARY'S MOURNING

In her first clinical consultation following the loss of her husband 9 months previously, Mary described John's death as "the gut-ripper of her life," the worst of a cascade of losses that had clustered in the last year. Although John had been troubled by vague and misdiagnosed symptoms for a few months, the actual diagnosis of metastatic bone cancer preceded his death by a mere 3 weeks. As a consequence, she said she felt "totally unprepared" for the loss of "the man who had been everything to me—my North, my South, my East, and my West." Most of all, Mary felt that with John's death she had lost her "anchor" in the world and, perhaps significantly in view of the cause of his death, describes her ongoing grief as "bone-shattering." She literally had been counting the days since his death and had never missed a single day of visitation to his graveside in a cemetery over an hour from her home, even in forbidding winter weather that made the drive a life-threatening proposition.

The special intimacy that Mary and John shared through 15 years of marriage contrasted sharply with the "miserable" first marriages each had endured previously. Mary described John as a perfect partner: devoted, good-humored, an excellent provider, and her "buffer" from a harsh world. Now she felt a keen sense of abandonment by the man who promised he would "always be there" in times of need, and subsequently had to cope with the death of her mother, who succumbed to advanced Alzheimer's, and her beloved aunt, who died of breast cancer, within 3 months of John's death. As a consequence, she has felt vulnerable and alone, a feeling that had heightened in the context of an angry legal battle with family members over her husband's estate. This dispute, as well as the general societal pressure she felt "to be over it," has left her embittered and distrustful of the intentions of others.

At the time of the interview, Mary only experienced any respite from her grief when she sensed John's "presence." Her desperate yearning for contact with him was reflected in her hysterical attempt to climb into John's open casket at the funeral and her still-frequent calls to their answering machine "just to hear his voice." Sometimes this wished-for contact came in dreams, as she responded to the sound of his voice saying, "Honey, come snuggle up to me," or at night when she clearly felt his hand in hers. The most sustained sense of contact came during one of her daily visits to his grave, when she felt that the beautiful sunset, a flock of birds, and the whispering of his voice were signs of his heavenly existence. However, Mary shared that such moments accentuated the loss, as she awakened to the reality of his death. Accordingly, she ruminated frequently about death as a release from pain and about the heavenly reunion it could bring; but aside from the vague consideration of taking massive doses of the sleeping pills and anti-anxiety medication she had been prescribed, she had no clear plans to suicide.

Mary went on to say that she felt "so encased in grief" that she didn't even know who she was anymore. She saw no vestiges of the outgoing person she used to be and felt enraged that "God would leave me here without any purpose for being left behind." Nothing about her present life made sense to her; as she summed it up, "the quality of my life is gone, and nothing is left but garbage." In her own words, she "couldn't accept that John is gone" and was left "in shock after losing the foundation he provided." In many ways she felt much like she did 9 days after his death rather than how she had hoped to feel a full 9 months later.

Even with these many problems, Mary did have some resources. She had somehow managed to keep her sales job in the insurance industry, even with a visible deterioration in her performance, and "kept up appearances" despite her 20-pound weight loss, frequent sleeplessness, and pervasive sadness and anger. Her adult son and daughter from her previous marriage were as attentive as possible, although neither lived nearby. Perhaps because of her absorption in her marriage, she had "given up all other friends," even prior to John's death. She did show a spark of pride, however, in producing a handsome laminated memorial card for John that she designed, which she spoke hopefully of using as the starting point for a book about him and about their relationship. She didn't want the memory of John to be "erased," and she somehow hoped that such a project would help her "get back some of the person she used to be."

WHEN GRIEF IS COMPLICATED

Bearing in mind the criteria for complicated grief (Shear et al., 2011), alternatively termed prolonged grief disorder (Prigerson et al., 2009), Mary clearly meets criteria for a marked and intense preoccupation with the loss of her husband, to a degree that greatly limits her ability to function in important social and occupational roles. She also struggles with a diminished sense of self, inability to accept the reality of the death, social estrangement, pervasive bitterness over the loss, difficulty "moving on" in a changed world, and confronting a future seemingly devoid of purpose. As she herself summed it up, her "quality of life" apparently died with John, and she feels vulnerable, disoriented, anguished, and alone, with the passage of time merely confirming her decimation rather than assuaging it.

Our goal in this chapter is to review briefly some of what is known about those factors that predispose people to intense, life-vitiating, and sometimes seemingly perpetual grieving, considering (a) the circumstances of the death, (b) the background of the bereaved, (c) their relationship to the deceased, (d) their styles of coping with the loss, and (e) the broader social and institutional systems in which they are engaged. A more exhaustive review of the many studies to date that have addressed risk factors in bereavement was provided more formally in our previous systematic summary of 43 prospective studies of 60 different possible predictors of bereavement outcome (Burke & Neimeyer, 2012). Here we will summarize some of the key findings of that review and add representative recent studies that confirm and extend these findings.

Circumstances of the death

Cause of death

Several studies that have examined cause of death as a risk factor have found no differences in complicated grief symptomatology as a function of whether the death resulted from natural or violent causes.

However, of those studies in which cause of death was a predictor, violent death was consistently found to produce more intense and complicated grief than deaths due to illness. Cleiren (1993) found that unnatural deaths (suicide/accident versus extended illness) led to more intense grief in parents and spouses and that suicide survivors were the most preoccupied with their loss. Gamino, Sewell, and Easterling (2000) compared 85 survivors of illness, homicide, suicide, and accident, and found that traumatic deaths produced more grief. Likewise, Currier, Holland, Coleman, and Neimeyer's (2007) investigation of 1,723 bereaved college students indicated that homicide survivors had more severe grief than those without an objectively traumatizing loss. Similarly, Keesee, Currier, and Neimeyer (2008) found more complicated grief in violently bereaved parents than in parents bereaved by other means. In the context of genocide, both Momartin, Silove, Manicavasagar, and Steel's (2004) study of Bosnian refugees exposed to multiple traumas and Dusingizemungu and Elbert's (2010) study of Rwandan survivors of ethnic massacre documented the link between the traumatic loss of a family member to homicide and the subsequent development of complicated grief. However, possibly because of the extremely traumatic nature of the violent deaths witnessed (for example, seeing one's loved ones dismembered by machete), the latter study found that other potential predictors (gender of the survivor, number of losses, participation in the funeral) bore no relation to bereavement outcome. In summary, although coping with the gradual death of a loved one by wasting illness poses its own bereavement risks, in general, sudden, violent losses that leave no time to say goodbye, commonly are premature, often entail complicated questions of human intention or inattention, routinely elicit existential queries lacking answers, and are frequently horrific or shocking, generally set the stage for prolonged, painful, and preoccupying grief.

Peri-event variables

Beyond the cause of the death per se, a few studies have identified other circumstances associated with the death itself that pose bereavement risk for survivors. In one study of 540 parents bereaved by the suicide of a child, Feigelman, Jordan, and Gorman (2009) found that those who found or saw the body at the scene of death experienced significantly greater grief than survivors who did not and that this proved to be the strongest risk factor for intense grief. These results essentially replicated the major finding of an earlier study by Callahan (2000), who reported that finding the body and seeing it at the scene of the death were equally potent in intensifying grief. However, grief was not increased by viewing the deceased's body at the funeral. A distinctive conclusion of the study was that the specific suicide method or weapon type used was not associated with grief outcomes, even when comparing the use of guns (the most common suicide method in the sample) to seven other methods. Troubling images and emotions associated with viewing a disturbing scene of death certainly are not limited to suicide loss, however, as they are also likely to occur in circumstances of homicide, accidents, and natural disasters. Moreover, occasional findings such as those linking a patient's quality of death in end-of-life contexts with better bereavement outcomes for survivors (Garrido & Prigerson, 2014) suggest that peri-event variables deserve closer study across a wider range of contexts, including deaths through progressive illness.

Background of the bereaved

Gender

Perhaps because it is an easily accessible demographic variable, gender is a frequently studied risk factor for complicated grief. For example, Lang and Gottlieb's (1993) study of parents whose infants had died found that mothers suffered the most in terms of grief. Spooren, Henderick, and Jannes (2000) found that although mothers and fathers bereaved by motor vehicle accidents did not differ in terms of their general psychological distress, gender did predict intense grief, with women suffering greater complications. In the Keesee et al. (2008) study, mothers reported more general grief than fathers but not more complicated grief (see also Schwab, 1996). Likewise, female Pakistani psychiatric patients in Prigerson et al.'s (2002) study had higher rates of complicated grief than did males. A large population-based study of German respondents suffering a variety of losses through bereavement likewise confirmed that female gender predicts greater complication (Kersting, Brähler, Glaesmer, & Wagner, 2011). More detailed analyses suggest that these gender differences are clinically as well as statistically significant. For example, Chiu et al. (2010) found that, among a large group of caregivers of loved ones with terminal cancer, women had more than double the risk of complicated grief, and Cohen-Mansfield, Shmotkin, Malkinson, Bartur, and Hazan (2013) found that mothers relative to fathers were at greater risk of premature mortality in the 20 years following the death of a child. However, other studies have found gender to be unrelated to grief (Boelen, van den Bout, & van den Hout, 2003; Ingram, Jones, & Smith, 2001; Neimeyer, Baldwin, & Gillies, 2006). Nonetheless, when gender differences are observed, as they often are, evidence indicates that women are more susceptible to intense and complicated grief reactions than men. More research is clearly needed to explain this effect, which could stem from gender differences established by biological, relational, sociological, or cultural factors.

Demographic disadvantage

Though less frequently studied, economic and educational resources could also play a role in complicating people's adjustment to loss. Burke and colleagues (2015) found higher levels of anguishing anticipatory grief among family members of patients in palliative care in those families with less formal education and lower incomes, whereas those with higher educational and economic status reported less distress. Lower income was likewise a risk factor for complicated grief in the large German study mentioned earlier (Kersting et al., 2011), and fewer years of education predicted worse grief among hospice caregivers of cancer patients a year following the death (Allen, Haley, Small, Schonwetter, & McMillan, 2013). Such socioeconomic disadvantage could also play a role in explaining some ethnic differences in bereavement complication. For example, in the United States, higher levels of complicated grief symptoms are reported by African Americans as opposed to Caucasians (Laurie & Neimeyer, 2008). Although the interpretation of these differences remains to be established, it is possible that having fewer economic resources aggravates the financial burdens associated with death (especially the death of the primary breadwinner), and that lower levels of education impose restrictions on the "medical literacy" of family members in understanding or negotiating treatment options provided to their loved ones in end-of-life settings (Burke et al., 2015).

Relationship to the deceased

Kinship

Other factors being equal, closer degrees of kinship to the deceased predict intensified grief (Boelen et al., 2003; Goldsmith, Morrison, Vanderwerker, & Prigerson, 2008; van der Houwen et al., 2010). For example, Laurie and Neimeyer's (2008) sample of 1,670 bereaved college students reported a main effect for kinship in predicting complicated grief symptoms, such that students who had lost immediate family had more grief than those bereaved of more distant relationships. Differences among kinship categories within the family are often observed as well. In Cleiren's (1993) study, kinship proved the strongest predictor of grief, with parents and spouses grieving more severely than children or siblings. Prigerson et al. (2002) similarly found that spouses and parents were far more likely (22 and 11 times, respectively) to have complicated grief than other kinship types. This finding (that death of a partner or child functions as a risk factor for difficulties in bereavement) has been replicated in large-scale studies in Australia (Aoun et al., 2015), China (Chiu et al., 2010), Germany (Kersting et al., 2011), and Israel (Cohen-Mansfield et al., 2013), suggesting that this pattern holds across cultures. Very probably this reflects the typical strength of the attachment bond between the survivor and the deceased, a factor considered in greater detail in the sections to follow.

Marital dependency

Two studies drawing on the same data set link dependency on a spouse to more intense and prolonged grief. Studying widowed persons in later life, Bonanno et al. (2002) reported that pre-loss spousal dependency was associated with subsequent chronic grieving. Similarly, Carr (2004) found that spousal dependency was a risk factor for despair, a specific dimension of grief. Converging with these conclusions, family members who cared for loved ones on whom they greatly depended have reported both more intense anticipatory grief in the context of palliative care (Burke et al., 2015) and more complicated grieving in subsequent adjustment to bereavement (Thomas, Hudson, Trauer, Remedios, & Clarke, 2014). Although dependency on a partner has many dimensions (financial support, social identity as a married person, etc.), the degree to which the surviving spouse had relied on the dying or deceased partner for emotional security seems to play a pivotal role. For example, van Doorn, Kasl, Beery, Jacobs, and Prigerson (1998) found that the loss of a security-enhancing relationship with the spouse put survivors at risk for greater complicated grief. Such findings suggest the relevance of examining more closely the character of the attachment bond or attachment style associated with more intense and preoccupying mourning, a topic to be considered in a later section.

Caregiver burden

Especially in the context of progressive illness such as cancer, dementia, AIDS, cystic fibrosis, and chronic obstructive pulmonary disease (COPD), family caregivers play a front-line role in attending to the needs of a loved one over the course of many months or years, often under accumulating emotional distress as the condition worsens. In addition to the ongoing risk of burnout during the illness, growing evidence suggests that caregiver burden also poses a risk for poor bereavement adjustment far beyond the death of the patient. For example, Thomas et al. (2014) found that those family members who had been primary caregivers for their spouses with cancer fared worse in bereavement than those without this responsibility, just as Chiu and colleagues (2010) discovered a link between a longer duration of caregiving and vulnerability to complicated grief. Similarly, Schulz, Boerner, Shear, Zhang, and Gitlin (2006) documented that pre-loss reports of caregiver burden among family members of dementia patients predicted higher levels of complicated grief 6 to 18 months later. Kapari, Addington, and Hotopf (2010) studied caregivers of patients with advanced disease of various kinds and reported that those who felt more burdened by the role during the caregiving phase also struggled more during their subsequent bereavement. Thus, it appears that the strain of caregiving, possibly in combination with related factors such as relentless exposure to the loved one's diminishment and the caregiver's ultimate inability to reverse the course of the illness, represents a significant risk factor for complicated grief. Of course, absorption in this role may well exacerbate distress by contributing to social isolation or neglect of other family relationships, factors related to our review of research on social support below.

Coping style

Attachment style

Of the factors determining human behavior under the stress of bereavement, the natural human orientation to develop emotional attachments to others may be among the most fundamental. Classically, Bowlby (1980) studied the relation between young children and their parents in stressful situations and identified those whose attachments were *secure*, that is, who displayed comfort with both seeking support from the parent in her presence and pursuing independent behavior in her absence. In contrast, children with an *insecure* style tended either to show fearful clinging when threatened with separation (anxious, dependent attachment) or compulsive self-reliance and indifference (avoidant attachment). A large number of studies have documented that these styles, rooted in early relationships with parents, tend to influence people's general responses to later circumstances that portend loss, including bereavement (Kosminsky & Jordan, 2016). For example, Johnson, Zhang, Greer, and Prigerson (2007) concluded that widows who recalled having a more "controlling" parent during their childhood developed greater dependency on their spouses in adult life and, consequently, more complicated grief following loss of that security-enhancing relationship. More specifically, van der Houwen et al. (2010) found that both anxious and avoidant attachment predicted complicated grief, although Meier, Carr, Currier, and Neimeyer (2103) found this association held most clearly for those insecure attachment patterns characterized by anxiety as opposed to avoidance. Tracing the impact of this risk factor over time, Brown, Nesse, House, and Utz (2009) found that insecure attachment style and grief were related at 6, 24, and 48 months following the death, suggesting its potency. In two studies, Wijngaards-de Meij and his colleagues (2007a; 2007b) showed that avoidant/anxious attachment styles explained 13% of the variance in complicated grief and that attachment coupled with neuroticism (or anxiety proneness) explained 22%. Interestingly, in their study of adjustment to impending loss at the end of life, van Doorn et al. (1998) found that insecure attachment uniquely predicted complicated grief as distinct from depression, reinforcing the conceptualization of this attachment style as a specific risk factor for maladaptive grief. However, this claim is qualified by the finding of Wayment and Vierthaler (2002), who found attachment anxiety to be associated with greater levels of both grief and depression and attachment avoidance to be predictive of somatization. At present, the safest conclusion is that insecure attachment, particularly of an anxious, dependent type, predisposes survivors to more difficult adjustment in bereavement, with complicated grief being among the most troubling outcomes.

Meaning making

A second major model bearing on coping with bereavement focuses on meaning reconstruction, namely the proposition that grieving entails a process of reaffirming or reconstructing a world of meaning that has been challenged by loss (Neimeyer, 2006). The bereaved commonly struggle with two key narrative tasks as they attempt to weave the reality of the death of a loved one into their life story. On the one hand, they attempt to process the "event story" of the death, the how and why of its occurrence, and what it means for their own lives going forward. On the other hand, they attempt to access the "back story" of the life of the deceased in order to reaffirm their bond, regain access to consoling memories, and reflect on the relevance of the relationship for their current and future selves (Neimeyer & Thompson, 2014). When the loss is seamlessly and perhaps straightforwardly integrated into the survivor's meaning system, the result is adaptive grief or resilience, whereas when the mourner struggles mightily to make sense of the loss and of his or her life in its wake, complicated, prolonged grief is assumed to ensue.

A great deal of empirical work supports this proposition. An unresolved search for meaning has been implicated in complicated grief outcomes in populations as diverse as young adults contending with a wide range of losses, middle-aged parents struggling with the loss of a child, and survivors of violent death bereavement resulting from suicide, homicide, and fatal accident (Neimeyer, 2016a). For example, Burke and her colleagues (2015) found that an inability to integrate the looming loss of a terminally-ill family member into the survivor's meaning system was the leading predictor of anguished anticipatory grief, accounting for more of the variance in the latter outcome than other important risk factors such as dependency on the dying patient, demographic disadvantage, and spiritual struggle. Similarly, Coleman and Neimeyer (2010) documented that an ongoing and unresolved search for meaning in the death of an elderly spouse at 6 and 18 months post-loss predicted more intense grief, whereas ability to make sense of the death at 6 months predicted psychological well-being a full 4 years beyond the loss. In short, a struggle to find sense or significance in the loss can be regarded as an early risk factor for prolonged and preoccupying grief, which takes on great practical importance insofar as it is one of only a few such factors that is modifiable through a large range of therapeutic interventions (Neimeyer, 2012, 2016b; Thompson & Neimeyer, 2014).

Social systemic and institutional factors

Social support

In the context of bereavement, social support can mean many things, including access to a confidante who can listen to one's distress without

---

judgment, the provision of respite in the form of companionship for enjoyable activities, or assistance with practical tasks and demands (Doka & Neimeyer, 2012). Recent research suggests that deficits in the latter area, such as a shortfall in support for child care and other instrumental tasks of living, can constitute a particularly significant risk factor for complicated grief, at least in the case of homicide bereavement (Bottomley, Burke, & Neimeyer, 2015). More generally, however, research indicates that the perceived absence of support for a particular griever within the family system (Chiu et al., 2010) or in the broader social network (Allen et al., 2013; Aoun et al., 2015; Kersting et al., 2007) places the person at risk for complicated grief, as do negative, intrusive, or critical responses from family and peers (Burke, Neimeyer, & McDevitt-Murphy, 2010). Placing such findings against the backdrop of evidence that poor family communication and functioning sets the stage for more problematic bereavement (Kissane & Parnes, 2014; Thomas et al., 2014), it is clear that social and systemic risk factors deserve greater attention in a field that is too exclusively preoccupied with individual vulnerabilities to complicated grief.

Institutional factors

All deaths happen somewhere, but where they occur and how relevant people and policies respond to losses in a given context are commonly neglected in the study of bereavement risk. Some research is beginning to suggest that the location of death itself can serve as a marker for greater difficulties in bereavement, whether in hospice (Chiu et al., 2010), home, or hospital (Aoun et al., 2015). The relative lack of informational and emotional support for family members in such settings could be one critical contributor to later bereavement complications. For example, Downar, Barua, and Sinuff (2014) discovered that nearly 70% of families losing a loved one in intensive care yearned to receive more support, and over half expressed a strong willingness to meet with the medical team to review events surrounding the death, perhaps suggesting a need for tangible informational assistance with making sense of the event. In the rather different context of suicide bereavement, family members have indicated that the performance of a "psychological autopsy," that is, of a systematic reconstruction with a professional of the psychological state and behavior of the decedent at the time of the suicide, is considered not merely educational, but also therapeutic by survivors (Henry & Greenfield, 2009). Risk factors associated with disengagement by professionals in various institutional roles and settings therefore can be ameliorated by offers to provide this sort of informational as well as emotional support at a painful juncture when both are greatly needed.

CONCLUSION AND RECOMMENDATIONS

In this chapter we have surveyed research on many of the prominent risk factors for complicated, prolonged grief, concentrating on several features of the circumstances of the death and background of the mourner, including his or her relation to the deceased, coping styles, and larger social system. Even with enumerating these categories and their various subcategories, however, the list of risk factors here cannot claim to be exhaustive, as additional sources of vulnerability have been documented in at least preliminary form, such as a history of mental health issues, particularly depression (Chiu et al., 2010; Schulz et al., 2006); spiritual struggle (Burke & Neimeyer, 2014; Burke, Neimeyer, McDevitt-Murphy, Ippolito, & Roberts, 2011); a history of unresolved loss (Chaurand, Feixas, Neimeyer, Salla, & Trujillo, 2015); and avoidant emotional coping (Schneider, Elahi, & Gray, 2007). As research on bereavement continues to evolve, this list of vulnerability markers is likely to grow in the years to come.

But beyond the documentation of vulnerability markers in any given case, a few points deserve emphasis. First, no risk factor occurs in isolation; any given mourner of any given loss might be characterized by none, a few, or many of them. For example, in the earlier case study, Mary's situation was characterized by several such factors: She was female, was losing her life partner, displayed a high degree of marital dependency upon John, and experienced a profound crisis of meaning in connection with his death. On the other hand, she also likely was buffered by the absence of other vulnerabilities, which might appropriately be seen as protective factors: She was relatively well-educated and affluent, was losing a spouse in the context of illness (although with a shockingly sudden trajectory from diagnosis to death), and had not contended with a long and exhausting period of caregiving and treatment. Other factors, such as the security of her early attachments, the quality of her social relations, and the level of informational support she received from medical caregivers, were more ambiguous. Ultimately her adaptation emerged in the context of all of these challenges and supports, though it was irreducible to any of them. In the end, her course through bereavement was determined by her initiatives to make sense of her loss and find her way back to a life that had meaning, buttressed by her faith, her family, and the support of caring others, including her grief therapist. Thus, risk factors alone are only part of the constellation of variables that shape people's adaptation to loss, and very little is known at present about how they interact with one another or with adaptive processes in the client and his or her social world.

Second, although grieving clearly plays out on levels ranging from the neurophysiological through the personal and relational to the more broadly social and cultural spheres of human activity (Neimeyer, Klass, & Dennis, 2014), the study of risk factors largely has been confined to an individualistic/personal level, with a modest concession to the role of broader contexts in the form of evaluation of the role of social support. But in an expanded model, complications in grieving might be understood to arise on the interfaces of different systems levels, that is, in conflicts or tensions between a given person and his or her family, between a family's response to the loss and the expectations of the broader community, or in the mismatch between one's personal means of coping and the cultural prescriptions applied to a person's gender, category of relationship to the deceased, or cause of death (Doka, 2002; Doka & Martin, 2010; Neimeyer & Jordan, 2002). Because these larger social dimensions of grieving have been given short shrift by researchers following a principally medical model of bereavement, it necessarily falls on clinicians to weigh intuitively the many factors that play into a given person's or family's vulnerability to complication and to decide which should be given the greatest attention.

Finally, it is worth emphasizing that however useful the identification of risk factors may be in helping determine bereaved people who may benefit from greater levels of support or professional assistance, such factors are commonly not modifiable by intervention (e.g., gender, economic disadvantage, kinship to the deceased, cause of death). However, some evidence-based risk factors are highly modifiable by treatment (e.g., meaning making, social support, specific coping strategies, and perhaps even attachment-related coping styles), suggesting their high relevance not only to the identification of those mourners who might benefit from treatment, but also to the selection of relevant goals and methods in grief therapy. We hope the current review and ongoing efforts to refine and assess risk factors for complication in bereavement helps readers pursue both of these goals with greater clarity.

Robert A. Neimeyer, PhD, *is a Professor of Psychology at the University of Memphis, where he also maintains an active clinical practice. Neimeyer has published 30 books, including* Techniques of Grief Therapy: Creative Practices for Counseling the Bereaved *and* Grief and the Expressive Arts: Practices for Creating Meaning, *the latter with Barbara Thompson, and serves as editor of the journal* Death Studies. *Neimeyer served as President of the Association for Death Education and Counseling (ADEC) and Chair of the International Work Group for Death, Dying, and Bereavement. In recognition of his scholarly contributions, he has been granted the Eminent Faculty Award by the University of Memphis, made a Fellow of the Clinical Psychology Division of the American Psychological Association, and given Lifetime Achievement Awards by ADEC and the International Network on Personal Meaning.*

Laurie A. Burke, PhD, *is a licensed clinical psychologist who maintains an active private practice in Portland, OR, that is dedicated to serving grieving individuals, with a primary focus on assisting traumatically bereaved adults (i.e., individuals grieving losses from homicide, suicide, or fatal accident). She received her doctorate in Clinical Psychology at the University of Memphis where she continues to conduct bereavement research as an assistant research professor. Dr. Burke's research and publications bear on death, dying, loss, and grief processes, with an emphasis on violent death bereavement, complicated grief, and complicated spiritual grief (CSG), which is a spiritual crisis following loss reflected in the griever's struggle with God and/or his or her spiritual community. Dr. Burke, who is one of the leading experts in the study of CSG, led the development and validation of the* Inventory of Complicated Spiritual Grief (ICSG), *and is presently testing a revised version, the* ICSG-R.

REFERENCES

Allen, J. Y., Haley, W. E., Small, B.J., Schonwetter, R. S., & McMillan, S. C. (2013). Bereavement among hospice caregivers of cancer patients one year following loss: Predictors of grief, complicated grief, and symptoms of depression. *Journal of Palliative Medicine, 16*(7), 745-751.

Aoun, S. M., Breen, L. J., Howting, D. A., Rumbold, B., McNamara, B., & Hegney, D. (2015). Who needs bereavement support? A population based survey of bereavement risk and support need. *PloS one, 10*(3), e0121101

Boelen, P. A., van den Bout, J., & van den Hout, M. A. (2003). The role of negative interpretations of grief reactions in emotional problems after bereavement. *Journal of Behavior Therapy and Experimental Psychiatry, 34*, 225-238.

Bonanno, G. A., Wortman, C. B., Lehman, D. R., Tweed, R. G., Haring, M., Sonnega, J.,...Nesse, R. M. (2002). Resilience to loss and chronic grief. *Journal of Personality and Social Psychology, 83*, 1150-1164.

Bottomley, J. S., Burke, L. A., & Neimeyer, R. A. (2015). Domains of social support that predict bereavement distress following homicide loss: Assessing need and satisfaction. *OMEGA—Journal of Death and Dying.* doi: DOI: 10.1177/0030222815612282

Brown, S. L., Nesse, R. M., House, J. S., & Utz, R. L. (2009). Religion and emotional compensation: Results from a prospective study of widowhood. *Society for Personality and Social Psychology, 30*, 1165-1174.

Bowlby, J. (1980). *Loss: Sadness and depression* (Vol. 3). New York, NY: Basic Books.

Burke, L. A., & Neimeyer, R. A. (2014). Complicated spiritual grief I: Relation to complicated grief symptomatology following violent death bereavement. *Death Studies, 38*, 259-267. doi: 10.1080/07481187.2013.829372

Burke, L. A., & Neimeyer, R. A. (2012). Prospective risk factors for complicated grief: A review of the empirical literature. In M. Stroebe, H. Schut, P. Boelen, & J. Van den Bout (Eds.), *Complicated grief: Scientific foundations for health care professionals* (pp. 145-161). Washington, DC: American Psychological Association.

Burke, L. A., Neimeyer, R. A., & McDevitt-Murphy, M. E. (2010). African American homicide bereavement: Aspects of social support that predict complicated grief, PTSD and depression. *OMEGA— Journal of Death and Dying, 61*, 1-24.

Burke, L. A., Neimeyer, R. A., McDevitt-Murphy, M. E., Ippolito, M. R., & Roberts, J. M. (2011). Faith in the wake of homicide: Spiritual crisis and bereavement distress in an African American sample. *International Journal for the Psychology of Religion, 21*, 289-307.

Burke, L. A., Clark, K. A., Ali, K. S., Gibson, B. W., Smigelsky, M. A., & Neimeyer, R. A. (2015). Risk factors for anticipatory grief in family members of terminally ill veterans receiving palliative care services. *Journal of Social Work in End-of-Life & Palliative Care.* 11:3-4, 244-266, doi: 10.1080/15524256.2015.1110071

Callahan, J. (2000). Predictors and correlates of bereavement in suicide support group participants. *Suicide and Life Threatening Behavior, 30*, 104-124.

Carr, D. S. (2004). African American/Caucasian differences in psychological adjustment to spousal loss among older adults. *Research on Aging, 26*, 591-622.

Chaurand, A., Feixas, G., Neimeyer, R. A., Salla, M., & Trujillo , A. (2015). Historia de pérdidas y sintomatología depresiva [History of losses and depressive symptoms]. *Revista Argentina de Clínica Psicológica, 24*, 179-188.

Chiu, Y. W., Huang, C., Yin, S., Huang, Y., Chien, C., & Chuang, H. (2010). Determinants of complicated grief in caregivers who cared for terminal cancer patients. *Supportive Care Cancer*, 1321-1327.

Cleiren, M. (1993). *Bereavement and adaptation: A comparative study of the aftermath of death.* Washington, DC: Hemisphere.

Cohen-Mansfield, J., Shmotkin, D., Malkinson, R., Bartur, L. & Hazan, H. (2013). Parental bereavement increases mortality in older persons. *Psychological Trauma: Theory, Research, Practice, and Policy, 5*(1), 84-92.

Coleman, R. A., & Neimeyer, R. A. (2010). Measuring meaning: Searching for and making sense of spousal loss in later life. *Death Studies, 34*, 804-834.

Currier, J. M., Holland, J., Coleman, R., & Neimeyer, R. A. (2007). Bereavement following violent death: An assault on life and meaning. In R. Stevenson & G. Cox (Eds.), In *Perspectives on violence and death* (pp. 177-202). Amityville, NY: Baywood.

Doka, K. (2002). *Disenfranchised grief* (2nd ed.). Champaign, IL: Research Press.

Doka, K., & Martin, T. (2010). *Grieving beyond gender*. New York, NY: Routledge.

Doka, K., & Neimeyer, R. A. (2012). Orchestrating social support. In R.A. Neimeyer (Ed.), *Techniques of grief therapy: Creative practices for counseling the bereaved* (pp. 315-317). New York, NY: Routledge.

Downar, J., Barua, R., & Sinuff, T. (2014). The desirability of an Intensive Care Unit (ICU) clinician-led bereavement screening and support program for family members of ICU decedents (ICU Bereave). *Journal of Critical Care, 29*(2), 311.e319-311.e316

Dusingizemungu, J. P., & Elbert, T. (2010). Rates and risks for prolonged grief disorder in a sample of orphaned and widowed genocide survivors. *BMC psychiatry, 10*(1), 55.

Feigelman, W., Jordan, J. R., & Gorman, B. S. (2009). How they died, time since loss, and bereavement outcomes. *OMEGA—Journal of Death and Dying, 58*, 251-273.

Gamino, L. A., Sewell, K. W., & Easterling, L. W. (2000). Scott & White grief study phase 2: Toward an adaptive model of grief. *Death Studies, 24*, 633-660.

Goldsmith, B., Morrison, R. S., Vanderwerker, L. C., & Prigerson, H. (2008). Elevated rates of prolonged grief disorder in African Americans. *Death Studies, 32*.

Garrido, M. M., & Prigerson, H. G. (2014). The end-of-life experience: Modifiable predictors of caregivers' bereavement adjustment. *Cancer, 120*(6), 918-925.

Henry, M., & Greenfield, B. J. (2009). Therapeutic effects of psychological autopsies. *Crisis, 30*(1), 20-24.

Ingram, K. M., Jones, D. A., & Smith, N. G. (2001). Adjustment among people who have experienced AIDS-related multiple loss: The role of unsupportive social interactions, social support, and coping. *OMEGA—Journal of Death and Dying,* 287-309.

Johnson, J. G., Zhang, B., Greer, J. A., & Prigerson, H. G. (2007). Parental control, partner dependency, and complicated grief among widowed adults in the community. *Journal of Nervous and Mental Disease, 195*(1), 26-30.

Kapari, M., Addington, J., & Hotopf, M. (2010). Risk factors for common mental disorder in caregiving and bereavement. *Journal of Pain and Symptom Management, 40*(6), 844-856.

Keesee, N. J., Currier, J. M., & Neimeyer, R. A. (2008). Predictors of grief following the death of one's child: The contribution of finding meaning. *Journal of Clinical Psychology, 64,* 1-19.

Kersting, A., Brähler, E., Glaesmer, H., & Wagner, B. (2011). Prevalence of complicated grief in a representative population-based sample. *Journal of Affective Disorders, 131*(1), 339-343.

Kersting, A., Kroker, K., Steinhard, J., Ludorff, K., Wesselmann, U., & Ohrmann, P. (2007). Complicated grief after traumatic loss: A 14-month follow-up study. *European Archive of Psychiatry Clinical Neuroscience, 257,* 437-443.

Kissane, D. W., & Parnes, F. (Eds.). (2014). *Bereavement care for families.* New York, NY: Routledge.

Kosminsky, P., & Jordan, J. R. (2016). *Attachment informed grief therapy.* New York, NY: Routledge.

Lang, A., & Gottlieb, L. (1993). Parental grief reactions and marital intimacy following infant death. *Death Studies, 17,* 233-255.

Laurie, A., & Neimeyer, R. A. (2008). African Americans and bereavement: Grief as a function of ethnicity. *OMEGA—Journal of Death and Dying, 57,* 173-193.

Meier, A. M., Carr, D. R., Currier, J. M., & Neimeyer, R. A. (2013). Attachment anxiety and avoidance in coping with bereavement: Two studies. *Journal of Social and Clinical Psychology, 32*(3), 315.

Momartin, S., Silove, D., Manicavasagar, V., & Steel, Z. (2004). Complicated grief in Bosnian refugees. *Comprehensive Psychiatry, 45*(475-482).

Neimeyer, R. A. (2006). *Lessons of Loss* (2nd ed.). New York, NY: Routledge.

Neimeyer, R. A. (2016a). Meaning reconstruction in the wake of loss: Evolution of a research program. *Behaviour Change.* doi: 10.1017/bec.2016.4

Neimeyer, R. A. (Ed.). (2012). *Techniques of grief therapy: Creative practices for counseling the bereaved.* New York, NY: Routledge.

Neimeyer, R. A. (Ed.). (2016b). *Techniques of grief therapy: Assessment and intervention.* New York, NY: Routledge.

Neimeyer, R. A., Baldwin, S. A., & Gillies, J. (2006). Continuing bonds and reconstructing meaning: Mitigating complications in bereavement. *Death Studies, 30,* 715-738.

Neimeyer, R. A., & Jordan, J. R. (2002). Disenfranchisement as empathic failure. In K. J. Doka (Ed.), *Disenfranchised grief* (pp. 97-117). Champaign, IL: Research Press.

Neimeyer, R. A., Klass, D. , & Dennis, M. R. (2014). A social constructionist account of grief: Loss and the narration of meaning. *Death Studies*(38), 485-498.

Neimeyer, R. A., & Thompson, B. E. (2014). Meaning making and the art of grief therapy. In B. E. Thompson & R. A. Neimeyer (Eds.), *Grief and the expressive arts: Practices for creating meaning* (pp. 3-13). New York, NY: Routledge.

Prigerson, H., Ahmed, I., Silverman, G. K., Saxena, A. K., Maciejewski, P. K., Jacobs, S. C.,...Hamirani, M. (2002). Rates of risks of complicated grief among psychiatric clinic patients in Karachi Pakistan. *Death Studies, 26*, 781-792.

Prigerson, H. G., Horowitz, M. J., Jacobs, S. C., Parkes, C. M., Aslan, M., Goodkin, K.,...Maciejewski, P. K. (2009). Prolonged grief disorder: Psychometric validation of criteria proposed for DSM-V and ICD-11. *PLoS Medicine, 6*(8), 1-12.

Schulz, R., Boerner, K., Shear, K., Zhang, S., & Gitlin, L. N. (2006). Predictors of complicated grief among dementia caregivers: A prospective study of bereavement. *The American Journal of Geriatric Psychiatry, 14*(8), 650-658.

Schwab, R. (1996). Gender differences in parental grief. *Death Studies, 20*(2), 103-113.

Schneider, K., Elahi, J., & Gray, M. (2007). Coping style use predicts Posttraumatic Stress and Complicated Grief symptom severity among college students reporting a traumatic loss. *Journal of Counseling Psychology, 54*(3), 344–350.

Shear, M. K., Simon, N., Wall, M. , Zisook, S., Neimeyer, R. A., Duan, N.,...Keshaviah, A. (2011). Complicated grief and related bereavement issues for DSM-5. *Depression and Anxiety, 28*, 103-117.

Spooren, D. J., Henderick, H., & Jannes, C. (2000). Survey description of stress of parents bereaved from a child killed in a traffic accident.. *OMEGA—Journal of Death and Dying, 42*, 171-185.

Thomas, K., Hudson, P., Trauer, T., Remedios, C., & Clarke, D. (2014). Risk factors for developing prolonged grief during bereavement in family carers of cancer patients in palliative care: A longitudinal study. *Journal of Pain and Symptom Management, 47*(3), 531-541.

Thompson, B. E., & Neimeyer, R. A. (Eds.). (2014). *Grief and the expressive arts: Practices for creating meaning*. New York, NY: Routledge.

van Doorn, C., Kasl, S. V., Beery, L. C., Jacobs, S. C., & Prigerson, H. G. (1998). The influence of marital quality and attachment styles on traumatic grief and depressive symptoms. *The Journal of Nervous and Mental Disease, 186*(9), 566-573.

van der Houwen, K., Stroebe, M., Stroebe, W., Schut, H., van den Bout, J., & Wijngaards-de Meij, L. (2010). Risk factors for bereavement outcome: A multivariate approach. *Death Studies, 34*, 195-220.

Wayment, H. A., & Vierthaler, J. (2002). Attachment style and bereavement reactions. *Journal of Loss & Trauma, 7*(2), 129-149.

Wijngaards-de Meij, L., Stroebe, M., Schut, H., Stroebe, W., van den Bout, J., & Heijden, P. G. M. (2007b). Neuroticism and attachment insecurity as predictors of bereavement outcome. *Journal of Research and Personality, 41*, 498-505.

Wijngaards-de Meij, L., Stroebe, M., Schut, H., Stroebe, W., van den Bout, J., & Heijden, P. G. M. (2007a). Patterns of attachment and parents' adjustment to the death of their child. *Personality and Social Psychology Bulletin, 33*, 537.

CHAPTER 7

Complicated Grief in Children and Adolescents

David A. Crenshaw

Author's note: For ease of communication, the term "children" will be used in this chapter to refer to both children and adolescents.

The grief of children is complicated by a multiplicity of factors. Grief is complicated if the death is traumatic. Grief is complicated by developmental factors; preschool children, and especially infants and toddlers, cannot understand the realities of death and often expect the deceased person to reappear. Grief is complicated for children when they suffer complex trauma. Complex trauma is not only reflective of multiple trauma but trauma derived from multiple sources. A child, for example, can grow up in poverty, experience one or more traumatic deaths in the family, be exposed to domestic violence, or be surrounded by violence in the neighborhood or in school. The nature and extent of these different sources of loss can complicate the grieving process.

DEFINING COMPLICATED GRIEF

Even experienced practitioners agonize over the confusion of terms in the bereavement field. Is the concept of complicated grief, for example, the same as traumatic grief, or are they different concepts? This question was put to seasoned clinicians working in the bereavement field (Dyregrov & Dyregrov, 2013), and the study revealed that professionals struggled with defining complicated grief in children but agreed that adult criteria for the diagnosis of complicated grief were inappropriate for children. The experienced professionals also agreed that the major features of complicated grief were intensity, duration, and longevity of grief reactions. The survey identified traumatic and delayed or inhibited grief as major subtypes of complicated grief.

Risk factors

In a review of the literature on the effects of complicated grief in adolescents who had experienced the death of a sibling, Dickens (2014) asserted that among the risk factors for complicated grief were coping strategies of the parents, the number of years since the death, the type of death, family support systems and relationships, therapeutic interventions, developmental ages of the siblings at the time of death, and the issue of finding meaning in life following the death. Dickens argued that complicated grief resulting in the development of anxiety disorders and symptoms of posttraumatic stress disorder (PTSD) may arise if one or all of these risk factors are present. Conceptually, however, this view adds to the confusion because the risk factors cited for development of complicated grief are the same as those that predict the development of anxiety disorders and PTSD.

McClatchey, Vonk, Lee, and Bride (2014) attempted to clarify the confusion by noting that the concepts of traumatic grief and complicated grief are used by some authors interchangeably, while others make a distinction between the two. The authors studied a sample of 240 parentally bereaved children using the Extended Grief Inventory (EGI) and analyzed the data with the goal of determining if traumatic grief and complicated grief are the same or two different concepts. The analysis yielded support for viewing these conditions as related but separate. The study found that children's age, gender, and ethnicity were important predictors of traumatic grief, but only gender and violent death were predictors of complicated grief. Confusion in the literature persists, however, since it is well-known among practitioners that violent death is often a key factor in traumatic grief as well as complicated grief.

Lack of clarity in the literature was also highlighted in a review of the concept of complicated grief (Boerner, Mancini, & Bonanno, 2013), which showed that complicated grief has been confused with normative grief. Ongoing research by Bonanno (2009) has shown that normative grief has often been pathologized. His work has shown that resilience is often overlooked in the bereavement field and that longitudinal studies demonstrate that normative grief can assume multiple pathways and trajectories over time. Thus, complicated grief can be confused not only with traumatic grief but also with uncomplicated grief that persists over time but is not indicative of a pathological state or condition.

Diagnostic considerations

Other writers (van den Bout & Kleber, 2013) considered the consequences of including complicated grief as an official diagnosis in the *Diagnostic and Statistical Manual of Mental Disorders* (5th ed.; *DSM-5*; American Psychiatric Association [APA], 2013) in view of the field's experience with PTSD, which had been included in the *DSM-III* (APA, 1980) as an official psychiatric diagnosis. While there have been positive effects of the inclusion, including more study of PTSD and related trauma conditions, there has also been controversy and lack of clarity about diagnostic criteria, concerns about lack of clinical utility, and inadequate data on prevalence. In a similar way, while including complicated grief as an official diagnosis might lead to some positive change, it will undoubtedly also bring some negative consequences as well. The diagnostic criteria seem more clear for PTSD than those that currently exist for complicated grief. For example, one question that arises is whether to apply a diagnostic label to a condition that may, in some cases, be largely influenced by sociocultural factors. Dickens (2014), in her review of the literature, identified family and social support as one of the key predictors of complicated grief. Similarly, Doka (2002) elucidated the extreme lack of family, community, or cultural support in the form of disenfranchised grief.

As a practitioner, I have also encountered significant problems with the diagnosis of PTSD. The diagnosis, by definition, is not supposed to be assigned unless the symptoms persist more than 30 days, but it is also widely recognized that in many cases, PTSD symptoms clear within 90 days even without treatment. The major discontent I find with the concept of PTSD is that these usually short-term symptoms do not begin to adequately capture the experience of trauma, especially when it involves children exposed to interpersonal trauma, such as abuse, neglect, or exposure to domestic violence. The real devastation of interpersonal trauma in childhood is the shattering of their trust in relationships (especially close, intimate relationships) that may present problems for a lifetime. It is surprising that academic researchers pay so little attention to these longer-term effects, instead seemingly preoccupying themselves with evidence-based treatments that treat short-term symptoms, which tend to clear in a relatively brief time on their own.

One of the more prominent methods among short-term treatments of childhood traumatic grief is an empirically derived treatment known as Trauma-Focused Cognitive Behavioral Therapy (TF-CBT). In the original treatment model, a total of 16 sessions were proposed for addressing both the trauma and grief symptoms (Cohen & Mannarino, 2004). This protocol was developed for Type 1 (single event trauma) and suggested two sessions to develop the trauma narrative. The model, to its credit, includes a parental treatment component; but clearly in the case of Type 2 (repeated trauma or ongoing trauma or complex trauma), where the source of the trauma derives from maltreatment at the hands of caretakers, this brief treatment intervention is unlikely to be adequate. When the very person(s) expected to keep the child safe is the one terrorizing the child, it creates an extremely complex, bewildering, and confusing situation for the child. To the credit of Cohen and Mannarino, and their colleague Deblinger, the researchers clearly state that there is simply no substitute for clinical judgment (2006). These researchers and others have published more recent papers suggesting modifications of the original TF-CBT protocol to more adequately meet the challenges of ongoing trauma and complex trauma (Dorsey & Deblinger, 2012; Cohen, Mannarino, & Navarro, 2012; Kliethermes & Wamser, 2012).

Further research

Some of the confusion surrounding concepts in the bereavement field are evidenced by Goldman's (1996) guide to helping children with complicated grief. She delineated ways of helping children acknowledge and process complicated feelings of grief associated with loss due to suicide, homicide, AIDS, violence, and abuse. Goldman asserted that children who experience abandonment, neglect, and various forms of abuse or loss associated with socially stigmatized circumstances develop feelings of complicated grief that tend to block normal grief and mourning. This description almost exactly matches what is now referred to as childhood traumatic grief, but it also overlaps with Doka's (2002) concept of disenfranchised grief—grief that is not sanctioned or socially supported due to the stigmatizing circumstances of the death.

Concepts about complicated grief in children continued to blur as researchers expanded terms to encompass more circumstances. Webb (2002) wrote that the term complicated grief refers to mourning in which the mourner attempts to deny, repress, or avoid aspects of the loss, and holds onto and resists relinquishing the lost loved one. This description of complicated grief focuses on the intrapsychic and psychodynamic forces that interfere with accepting the loss. Webb presented a case study in which two sisters experienced the dual loss of their parents' separation and the death of their godfather. She explained that the term complicated grief in this context refers to the responses of the girls (ages 8 and 10) as they faced two simultaneous losses of important paternal figures in their lives. Thus, Webb uses the term to also characterize the response of children where the timing of the losses is a significant factor.

To complicate matters further, European writers in the bereavement field refer to a syndrome of disturbed grief called prolonged grief disorder (PGD) in both adults and children (Spuij, van Londen-Huiberts, & Boelen, 2013). These researchers contend that PGD in children and adults is a distinct syndrome separate from traumatic grief, but the evidence for this seemed controversial because one of the studies cited with adolescents (Melhem et al., 2004) described a traumatic grief reaction associated with increased suicidal ideation, depression, and PTSD. Likewise, studies by Brown and Goodman (2004) and Cohen and Mannarino (2004) were cited as additional support for PGD in adolescents being a separate disorder, but in fact these studies were in support of childhood traumatic grief. More recent research by Melhem, Porta, Payne, and Brent (2013) argues that there is a syndrome that applies to 10% of bereaved adults and 10% of children whose parent had died suddenly. They called this prolonged grief reaction and used the term interchangeably with complicated grief. The children in this study were suffering prolonged grief reactions nearly 3 years after the death of the parent. These investigators reported prolonged grief reaction to be associated with a three-fold increase in depression and worsening functional impairment at home, school, and with peers. While there is a well-known tendency in the mental health field to pathologize such reactions, it does not seem all that remarkable that 10% of children who experienced the sudden death of a parent would be significantly suffering nearly 3 years later. Does the field need a "new" syndrome, such as prolonged grief reaction or complicated grief, to explain such responses? It speaks to the resilience of children that 90% of them do not show such suffering, but is it helpful with respect to the 10% still suffering to create a new diagnostic classification?

The need for ongoing research

Complicated grief in childhood appears in the literature to be assumed to be connected to certain kinds of traumatic deaths, such as for children and adolescents who are family survivors of homicides (Vigil & Clements, 2003). While clinically there are many challenges and complications to treating child grievers who have experienced the homicide of a loved one, this is far from proving the case that such youth suffer a separate syndrome of complicated grief distinct from childhood traumatic grief.

Reflecting the confusion and lack of agreement about diagnostic terms, the most recent version of the *DSM-5* (APA, 2013) includes a classification named persistent complex bereavement disorder (PCBD), listed in Section III under the header of "Conditions for Further Study." This listing is not an official diagnostic category in the *DSM-5,* but it is anticipated that with more study and research, it may become one in future editions. Some research has noted that, although bereavement and a grief process naturally occurs not only in humans but also in some species of animals, approximately 10% to 12% of individuals suffer a prolonged grief reaction or complicated grief that does not naturally resolve. These people suffer a range of functional impairments, which are typically classified as prolonged grief disorder or complicated grief (in much of the literature, these terms appear to be interchangeable) and are often associated with detrimental long-term health effects (Prigerson et al., 2009). The variables that distinguish prolonged or complicated grief from what is considered normal bereavement are primarily intensity and duration. The American Psychiatric Association appears to have exercised appropriate caution in deciding that PCBD and complicated grief require further study before inclusion in the official *DSM*, based in part on the research of Bonanno (2009) that has delineated several trajectories of bereavement that can be considered within the range of human differences and normalcy. It should be noted that the conceptual confusion that pertains to complicated grief in adults is exacerbated when considering children because developmental factors impacting their cognitive and emotional capacities to grieve add to the lack of clarity.

While these controversies and confusions in terms of labeling may persist for at least the foreseeable future, there appears to be a small percentage of adults and children whose experience of grief is more intense and longer lasting than with the vast majority of grievers. Adequate treatment of these individuals, whether children or adults, is important because they may also be at risk for a range of other health problems including cancer and cardiac events (Lannen, Wolfe, Prigerson, Onelov, & Kreicbergs, 2008).

TRAUMA AND BEREAVEMENT

For both conceptual and clinical purposes, it is important for those treating children to distinguish between trauma and bereavement. A highly useful and pragmatic distinction was made by Raphael and Martinek (1997) in noting that trauma is indicated by intrusions, memories, and preoccupations with the scene of the trauma event, whereas in bereavement, the focus is primarily on the deceased loved one. In the case of traumatic bereavement, where both trauma and grief elements are present, the former may interfere with the grief process. Typically, in this case the trauma elements are addressed first, such as exposure treatments to deal with intrusive images, frequent and reoccurring nightmares, startle reactions, and sleep disturbances, before focusing on the grief components (Cohen & Mannarino, 2004). Unless the acute trauma symptoms are relieved, it may not be possible for children to tolerate focusing on their feelings of loss long enough to reap the benefit of doing so. Sometimes counselors will hear from clients that "talking about it just makes it worse" when it comes to bereavement counseling. This may be at least partially due to the fact that trauma elements, if present, have not been adequately addressed.

Complicated grief related to parental sudden death (Jeremiah, age 5)

Jeremiah was brought to my private practice during the beginning of his kindergarten year with symptoms of PTSD, including intrusive images, sleep problems, recurrent vivid nightmares, and startle reactions. Jeremiah's father had been murdered in an attempted robbery at the convenience store that he owned. His father was in his office in the back of the store when the attempted robbery took place; upon hearing the commotion he rushed out and was shot by one of the two masked men. Although Jeremiah did not directly witness the killing of his father, the intrusive images were so vivid that his suffering was akin to that of an eyewitness of the horrific event. Night after night following the homicide, Jeremiah fought going to bed because he did not want to close his eyes and see the images of his father being shot; these images intruded in his mind when he could not keep himself busy. Once in bed, he feared falling asleep because of the ongoing nightmares he had; they would cause him to scream out, awakening his mother and sister so that no one in the house could get a dependable night's sleep. Of course, his mother and sister were also in shock and grief-stricken, but were not suffering the same degree of PTSD symptoms as Jeremiah. The family was very close-knit, and although the extended family was extremely supportive, their well-intended efforts to console Jeremiah seemed to just make him miss his father even more.

While the family was loving and close, Jeremiah had been especially close to his father. Jeremiah's favorite activities with his dad were playing catch and fishing together. For weeks after his father's death, Jeremiah would sit in the living room with his baseball glove on, waiting for his father to come home. He simply could not accept the fact that his father was never coming home again. Acceptance of such a momentous loss is difficult in any circumstance, but at age 5, Jeremiah could resort to magical thinking and still anticipate that, just maybe, the next person coming through the door would be his father. The acceptance of such a loss is compounded when the death is sudden; the finality of the loss is difficult for any young child to comprehend. In addition to his trauma symptoms, not surprisingly, Jeremiah was quite angry that his father was taken away from him so suddenly and brutally, and at such a young age. Jeremiah frequently asked, "I hardly had time to get to know my dad; how could he be gone?" Jeremiah's anger surfaced frequently in temper outbursts both at school and at home. Sometimes the slightest frustration or annoyance would cause a destructive lashing out in rage that was sometimes startling to his teacher and classmates and deeply concerning to his mother, sister, and grandparents.

Jeremiah's anger was understandable, but as with many children at his age, he lacked the reliable emotional regulation capacity to channel it in more constructive ways. Typical of children his age, verbalizing his angry feelings was not his strong suit, so the challenge in therapy was to find ways that were developmentally sensitive to enable him to express the anger that intensely burned inside.

The therapy process

The research on psychotherapy clearly indicates that two of the most robust variables that determine successful outcomes are the resources that the client brings and the quality of the therapeutic relationship. Specific techniques and interventions that will be discussed in this section are viewed as secondary in importance to the two main influences of Jeremiah's personal resources consisting of, among other things, his intelligence, coping skills, and resilient traits, as well as the quality of the therapeutic relationship. Jeremiah was a bright child and a quick learner. The closeness to his family, both nuclear and extended, and particularly his affectionate relationship with his father, indicated a strong capacity for relationships with others. As a result, Jeremiah attached to me as his therapist as quickly as could be expected for a child who had just suffered the traumatic loss of his father. As an older male, a potential attachment figure in my role as therapist, some fear and caution was evident in the beginning on Jeremiah's part, as would be expected. But a bond was formed between us that he could rely on and turn to, even later at various points during his developmental years. Jeremiah shared a strong interest in sports and outdoor activities. On days when he could not tolerate exploring his feelings or focusing on his devastating loss, we would sometimes go outside for a walk, throw a ball in the office, or play a miniature tennis game. Jeremiah became skilled at pacing and distancing when he needed to, and I praised him for his ability to keep himself safe because nothing was more important than keeping the therapy safe. One of the most important concepts for therapists working with trauma events or complicated grief is the theory of "windows of affect tolerance" that Daniel Siegel (1999, 2012) articulated. Siegel explained that every person has a safe range (window) of intensity of affect that can be tolerated. If the intensity exceeds that window, however, the therapy/counseling becomes unsafe. Thus, the child may become overwhelmed; act out (such as run out of the room, become destructive, or refuse to come to the next session); and in extreme cases be traumatized or retraumatized. The challenge to the therapist is that the window of safe affect tolerance can vary from session to session or even in the same session depending on the focus and topics. The skills and experience of the therapist is tested to keep the therapeutic work safe; the requisite skill set includes timing, pacing, therapeutic presence, attunement, and unflinching empathy.

Specific interventions

Use of metaphor

In the beginning of therapy, I introduced the metaphor of the "Family Photo Album." I told Jeremiah to pretend that he was looking at a family photo album with his sister and mother.

> As you look at the album together, you turn the pages and you see pictures of you as an infant or small child being held and hugged by your parents and it brings back such warm feelings and memories. It reminds you of how much you were loved and cherished by your family when you came into this world and are still loved to this day. Then you turn the page to see more pictures of being loved and held by your parents, your sister, and your grandparents, confirming just how much you were loved and special to your family. Then you turn the page to see some pictures of family vacations where clearly everyone was having a good time and enjoying being together. These pictures bring back warm and happy memories but also the feeling of longing to have those good times back. You turn the page again, and this time there is a picture of you and your father playing catch together in the backyard. This picture makes you too sad. You decide to close up the album and put it back on the shelf. You tell your mom and sister that you will come back to it at a time that is more comfortable and better for you.

I explained to Jeremiah that we would proceed in the same way during our time together in therapy. I told him I would invite him to go as far as he could in expressing his sadness, his missing of his dad, his anger that his dad was taken from him, but when it became too much, when he felt too sad or too angry, we would stop and put it on the shelf, and come back to it at a time that is more comfortable for him. In terms of making the therapy safe for children who are in the throes of trauma experiences or acute pain, I've learned that both of the implied messages are important: "We will stop for now and put it away on the shelf" and "We will come back to it at a time that is more comfortable for you." The child realizes safety is important and we can pace the work so that it is not overwhelming, but we will also come back to it at a time that is more comfortable. Planting this firm expectation that we will come back and confront the "hard parts" is just as important a message as that we will go at a comfortable and safe pace.

Drawings

Since children have a hard time verbalizing the painful emotions of grief or traumatic events, some will do better drawing their feelings and memories. A favorite drawing strategy is to ask the child to draw pictures of their happy memories involving their deceased loved one. Jeremiah liked to draw, so expressing his longing for his dad through drawings gave him enough safe distance to be able to express his pain and grief. He drew many pictures over six sessions, including playing ball and fishing with his dad or spending time on family vacations. One of Jeremiah's drawings included his father chasing him around the yard with a hose, which made him laugh. Humor has always been a good prognostic sign in my clinical experience. At one point, Jeremiah reflected on the substantial pile of drawings of happy memories and commented, "I guess I am lucky in a certain way because I have all the happy memories of my times together with my dad," adding that some kids have none or very few.

Drawings were also a useful tool in helping Jeremiah give safe, symbolic expression to his anger and rage. I asked him to pick from various figurative categories to symbolically express how angry he felt. The categories included volcanoes, storms, fire-breathing dragons, angry monsters, and raging bulls. I would direct Jeremiah, for example, to draw a volcano that would reflect how angry he felt that his father was murdered. He drew a volcano erupting with hot lava, threatening to destroy entire villages in its path. He also used other categories such as an angry monster, raging bull, or a hurricane to express his intense rage. Drawings not only symbolized his rage but also contained it in an artistic and creative expression.

Stories

Stories are another way to help children reflect on their own situation in a safe way. One of the stories I shared with Jeremiah was *The Three-Legged Dog* (Mills & Crowley, 1986, 2014). This story has proved to be a source of hope, comfort, and solace for many grieving children I've worked with. The story is about an actual experience recounted by Joyce Mills when she was driving one day with her son Casey in the backseat and saw a dog running with just three legs. Casey asked all kinds of questions about how the dog had lost a leg, but Mills explained to her son that "We don't know what happened to the dog, whether it was an accident or if it was born that way. The important thing is that the dog has learned to do on three legs what other dogs do on four legs" (Mills & Crowley, 2014, p. 58). This story has special meaning for Jeremiah, who right away commented, "We were once a four-legged family and now we are a three-legged family."

I shared another story with Jeremiah, from a story series developed to bring hope and comfort to grieving children called the *Bramley Rabbit Story Series* (Crenshaw & Crenshaw, 2006). Although the stories were not written with Jeremiah in mind, they resonated deeply with him, as they are about a rabbit who lost his father quite suddenly and the numerous challenges that followed. Along its journey, the rabbit finds some degree of peace and acceptance. In many cases, children are able to find elements in a story that relate to their own lives and own journey through grief and loss.

Developmentally sequenced grief work

All traumatic deaths during childhood can cause complicated grief (although there will always be exceptions) because the child developmentally is not cognitively, emotionally, or socially equipped to deal with such shattering losses. Children can be invited to go as far as they can at a given age, with the understanding that they may well need to revisit and regrieve their loss as they advance in their development and understand the meaning and the consequences of the loss better. Jeremiah returned to therapy at age 9 when he became more cognizant that death was final and irreversible, which ushered in a new period of grieving. He came back for more work when he was 14 after his first romance broke up suddenly and triggered feelings of his father's shocking death. Jeremiah returned to counseling for the final time when he graduated from high school and was overwhelmed with sadness that his father could not be there to celebrate this important accomplishment with him. Throughout his later childhood years and adolescence, his relationship with his mother and sister strengthened, and those bonds were instrumental in helping him bear the loss of his grandparents with whom he felt so close and attached. I heard from Jeremiah about 2 years ago. He had finished college and is now married with two young daughters; he is a proud and loving father and husband, just as his father was.

David A. Crenshaw, PhD, ABPP, RPT-S, is Clinical Director of the Children's Home of Poughkeepsie, NY, and adjunct assistant professor in the graduate clinical psychology program at Teachers College, Columbia University, and Marist College. He is a Board Certified Clinical Psychologist by the American Board of Professional Psychology, Fellow of the American Psychological Association (APA), and Fellow of APA's Division of Child and Adolescent Psychology. He is also a Registered Play Therapist-Supervisor (RPT-S) by the Association for Play Therapy. Dr. Crenshaw is a Past President of the New York Association for Play Therapy, and also the Hudson Valley Psychological Association, which honored him with its Lifetime Achievement Award in 2012. He has written or edited 12 books on child aggression, trauma, grief, and resilience, and over 50 book chapters and journal articles. His latest books are Play Therapy Interventions to Enhance Resilience, *co-edited with Robert Brooks and Sam Goldstein, and* Termination Challenges in Child Psychotherapy, *co-written with Eliana Gil.*

References

American Psychiatric Association. (2013). *Diagnostic and statistical manual of mental disorders* (5th ed.). Washington, DC: American Psychiatric Association.

Boerner, K., Mancini, A. D., & Bonanno, G. (2013). On the nature and prevalence of uncomplicated and complicated patterns of grief. In M. Stroebe, H. Schut, & J. van den Bout (Eds.), *Complicated grief: Scientific foundations for health care professionals* (pp. 55-67). New York, NY: Routledge/Taylor & Francis Group.

Bonanno, G. A. (2009). *The other side of sadness: What the new science of bereavement tells us about life after loss.* New York, NY: Basic Books.

Brown, E. J., & Goodman, R. F. (2005). Childhood traumatic grief: An exploration of the construct in children bereaved on September 11. *Journal of Clinical Child and Adolescent Psychology, 34,* 248–259. doi:10.1207/s15374424jccp3402_4

Cohen, J. A., & Mannarino, A. P. (2004). Treatment of childhood traumatic grief. *Journal of Clinical Child and Adolescent Psychology, 33*(4), 819-831.

Cohen, J. A., Mannarino, A. P., & Deblinger, E. (2006). *Treating trauma and traumatic grief in children and adolescents.* New York, NY: Guilford Press.

Cohen, J. A., Mannarino, A. P., & Navarro, D. (2012). TF-CBT setting applications: Residential treatment. In J. A. Cohen, A. P. Mannarino, & E. Deblinger (Eds.), *Trauma-focused CBT for Children and Adolescents* (pp. 73-104). New York, NY: Guilford Press.

Crenshaw, D. A., & Crenshaw, S. L. (2006). Bramley story series. In D. A. Crenshaw, *Evocative Strategies in Child and Adolescent Psychotherapy,* (pp. 41-51). Lanham, MD: Jason Aronson.

Dickens, N. (2014). Prevalence of complicated grief and posttraumatic stress disorder in children and adolescents following sibling death. *The Family Journal, 22*(1),119-126. http://dx.doi.org/10.1177/1066480713505066

Doka, K. (Ed.) (2002). *Disenfranchised grief: New directions, challenges, and strategies for practice.* Champaign, IL: Research Press.

Dorsey, S., & Deblinger, E. (2012). TF-CBT setting applications: Children in foster care. In J. A. Cohen, A. P. Mannarino, & E. Deblinger (Eds.), *Trauma-focused CBT for Children and Adolescents* (pp. 49-72). New York, NY: Guilford Press.

Dyregrov, A., & Dyregrov, K. (2013). Complicated grief in children: The perspectives of experienced professionals. *OMEGA—Journal of Death and Dying, 67*(3), 291-303.

Goldman, L. (1996). *Breaking the silence: A guide to helping children with complicated grief.* New York, NY: Routledge.

Kliethermes, M., & Wamser, R. (2012). TF-CBT setting applications: Adolescents with complex trauma. In J. A. Cohen, A. P. Mannarino, & E. Deblinger (Eds.), *Trauma-focused CBT for Children and Adolescents* (pp. 175-198). New York, NY: Guilford Press.

Lannen, P. K., Wolfe, J., Prigerson, H. G., Onelov, E. & Kreicbergs, U. C. (2008). Unresolved grief in a national sample of bereaved patients: Impaired physical and mental health 4 to 9 years later. *Journal of Clinical Oncology, 26*(36): 5870-5876.

McClatchey, I., Vonk, M., Lee, J., & Bride, B. (2014). Traumatic and complicated grief among children: One or two constructs? *Death Studies, 38*(2), 69-78.

Melhem, N. M., Day, N., Shear, M. K., Day, R., Reynolds, C. F., & Brent, D. (2004). Traumatic grief among adolescents exposed to a peer's suicide. *American Journal of Psychiatry, 161*, 1411–1416. doi:10.1176/appi.ajp. 161.8.1411

Melhem, N. M., Porta, G., Payne, M. W., & Brent, D. A. (2013). Identifying prolonged grief reactions in children: Dimensional and diagnostic approaches. *Journal of the American Academy of Child & Adolescent Psychiatry, 52*(6), 599-607.

Mills, J. C., & Crowley, R. J. (1986). *Therapeutic metaphors for children and the child within.* New York, NY: Bruner Mazel.

Mills, J. C., & Crowley, R. J. (2014). *Therapeutic metaphors for children and the child within. (2nd ed.).* New York, NY: Routledge.

Prigerson, H. G., Horowitz, M. J., Jacobs, S. C., Parkes, C. M., Aslan, M., Goodkin, K., Raphael, B., & Marwit, S. J. (2009). Prolonged Grief Disorder: Psychometric validation of criteria proposed for DSM-V and ICD-11. *PLoS Medicine, 6*(8): e100121

Raphael, B. & Martinek, N. (1997). Assessing traumatic bereavement and posttraumatic stress disorder. In J. Wilson and T. Keane, (Eds.), Assessing psychological trauma and PTSD (pp. 373-395). New York, NY: The Guilford Press.

Siegel, D. J. (1999). *The developing mind (1st ed.): How relationships and the brain interact to shape who we are.* New York, NY: Guilford Press.

Siegel, D. J. (2012). *The developing mind (2nd ed.): How relationships and the brain interact to shape who we are.* New York, NY: Guilford Press.

Spuij, M., van Londen-Huiberts, A., & Boelen, P. A. (2013). Cognitive-behavioral therapy for prolonged grief in children: Feasibility and multiple baseline study. *Cognitive and Behavioral Practice, 20*, 349-361.

Van den Bout, J., & Kleber, R. J. (2013). Lessons from PTSD for complicated grief as a new DSM disorder. In M. Stroebe, H. Schut, & J. Van den Bout (Eds.), *Complicated grief: Scientific foundations for health care professionals* (pp. 115-128). New York, NY: Routledge.

Vigil, G. J., & Clements, P. T. (2003). Child and adolescent homicide survivors: Complicated grief and altered worldviews. *Journal of Psychosocial Nursing & Mental Health Services, 41*, 30-39.

Webb, N.B. (Ed.). (2002). *Helping bereaved children: A handbook for practitioners*, 2nd ed. New York, NY: Guilford Press.

CHAPTER 8

The Dynamic Narrative Themes of Violent Dying in Grief

Edward Rynearson

Humans process and share emotive experience through stories; the readiness to tell one another stories is so pervasive we might be labeled *homo narran (story seeker)* rather than *homo sapien (knowledge seeker)*. Or perhaps it is through the creation of stories that we seek to know ourselves.

The intersection of attachment with dying and death is universal and timeless as a resource for story and storytelling. Dying and death introduce an antinarrative, a story without relational fulfillment. The inevitable death of someone intrinsic to one's private self, whether a parent, sibling, spouse, child, partner, best friend, or even a pet, triggers a private, introspective cascade of narrative remembrance of shared living. The story of such an attachment accompanies the signs and symptoms of bereavement and grief as an integral facet of a reorganizing pattern or "syndrome."

When dying is violent, from accident, suicide, homicide, genocide, or terrorism, the narrative reenactment of the dying may overshadow or eclipse the living narrative of the deceased. A therapeutic process of revising and restoring this narrative imbalance is here described.

To understand the centrality of story telling and retelling in "grief work" associated with violent dying, it is important to clarify the underlying structure of dying stories and their psychological purpose. Patients with dysfunctional grief after violent dying are challenged by narratives structured differently than the narrative remembrance commonly cited with complicated grief. In complicated grief, the narrative is generally an alluring story of resurrection and reunion with the deceased that denies and diverts from the dysphoria triggered by their absence. By contrast, retelling violent dying is an aversive, rather than an alluring, story containing themes of horror and helplessness, with counter themes of remorse, reenactment, retaliation, and retribution that distort the dying story structure (Rynearson, 2001; Currier, Holland, & Neimeyer, 2006).

This case study highlights this divergence. Mary, a 17-year-old student, is kidnapped while walking home from school. Her family maintains a desperate hope that she is safe and will be released, but weeks later, her body is discovered and an autopsy confirms she was raped and sodomized before being strangled to death. News of her disappearance and dying are widely publicized, including grisly televised images of the shallow grave where her body was found.

A month later police capture the murderer, a chronically psychotic man, and during his trial the family is forced to listen to details of the crime reconstructed from police and autopsy reports. Found not guilty by reason of insanity, the killer is committed to a local state hospital. The family organizes a memorial service in the school gymnasium under the glare of media cameras and reporters. Suspended over this community spectacle is the shadow of Mary's death, her victimization by the assailant, and the absence of retribution for the family by the justice system, all of which serve as a dark, unspoken counterpoint to the celebration of her life.

How different would be the story of Mary's dying and death for her family had it followed a natural death from a disease like cancer? The physical "forces" of natural dying are not readily capable of being storied in visual terms. Mary's cancer would be perceived as an internal, impersonal, biological aberrancy. Once diagnosed, Mary, her family, and the oncologists could play an active part in the unfolding narrative of her dying. At first, they were intent on rescuing her from dying with aggressive therapies; as the illness progressed, preparing Mary and themselves for her eventual death; and finally, being there as she died to ensure her comfort. She would not die alone, or in pain, or isolated from those who loved her. All of these caring enactments would be included in her natural dying narrative, creating a more acceptable and coherent "ending" for those bereaved, and her living memory would not be overshadowed by the way she died.

Unlike the internal biologic forces of natural dying, Mary's violent dying was an external act. Caused by a series of extrinsic, physical forces, the dying would be automatically storied as a visualized reenactment containing human character(s) in a plotting of entrapment. Her murder would be followed by a public response of widespread alarm and fear, police investigation, and trial. Because Mary's dying was unwitnessed (it is rare that anyone is present at the violent dying of a loved one), those bereaved would visually reconstruct her killing from media and police reports embellished by private and surreal fantasies of her terminal moments of isolated horror, helplessness, and agony. The family's retelling would be doubly confounded, powerless to have played a role in the unfolding story of her dying and powerless to control its public retelling.

Generally, the structure of the story of natural dying is linear and coherent with time and space for the bereaved to play an active role as a caring figure and supportive ally despite the mournful ending. In contrast, the structure of the story of violent dying is pulsating and unbearable with no time or space for the bereaved to play an active role as savior to reverse the horrific ending.

THE NARRATIVE FIXATIONS OF RESURRECTION AND REENACTMENT

The interruption of an attachment relationship evokes a compensatory story and retelling of the deceased to counterbalance their absence as if their "remembered" presence will rejoin a relationship that has been "dismembered." At first there is a simple recounting of the action of the dying and death to psychologically externalize the narrative through repetition and reexposure. The vivid imagery in this early recounting has a neurobiological correlate in the neurological model of "phantom" phenomena after the amputation of a limb (Flor et al., 1995). Despite its absence, the neural representation of an essential part of the body or "self" involuntarily registers as a continuing presence at a central level of consciousness. There are preliminary neuroimaging studies localizing cortical and subcortical areas of hyperreactivity associated with exposure to the image of the deceased in subjects with prolonged grief (Gundel, O'Connor, Littrell, Fort, & Lane, 2003); while these early reports of neurobiological changes are intriguing, they unfortunately have no clinical relevance or application. Within several months, neural reorganization spontaneously follows and the "phantom" of a severed limb or narratives of the dying and death of the deceased diminish, but remain implicit and never disappear.

However, in 10% to 20% of subjects with complicated grief these narratives associated with dying and death do not diminish but remain intense and are associated with dysfunction (Jacobs, 1999). When the narrative resurrection of the deceased persists, it is commonly cited as an obstacle to accommodation in patients with complicated grief. The resurrection fixation is theorized to be the product of an attachment vulnerability of anxious dependence. The dynamic basis of complicated grief purports that self-efficacy and stability is dependent on the proximity and caregiving of the deceased. Complicated grief is theoretically triggered by the finality of their absence, and is followed by traumatic separation distress and imagery of self-disintegration with compensatory reunion and revitalization fantasies, regardless of the mode of dying, natural or violent.

The patterns of narrative fixations after violent dying appear to be qualitatively different. Following violent dying, narratives of resurrection may similarly occur in those bereaved. However, after violent dying the bereaved is additionally challenged in processing the narrative reenactment of the externally induced dying. Since there can be no compensatory comfort, value, or meaning in the narrative of reenactment or its retelling, it cannot serve a compensatory function. The experiential elements of the violent dying (violence, violation, and volition) are aversive and incoherent, different than elements of the resurrection remembrance that are consoling and meaningful.

The fixation of narrative reenactment may be driven more by blocked assumptions of caregiving than care-receiving. The intense self-remorse after violent dying may be associated with the ultimate attachment obligation of providing safety for the deceased, creating an ensnaring riddle, i.e., "the safety of my loved one was my ultimate responsibility, so I cannot allow the dying to happen." This intense obligation of providing safety in the attachment relationship is commonly noted in parents of dependent children who die violently and, most particularly, in mothers.

The narrative elements of violent dying and remorseful entrapment are not ingredients of an energizing phantom of comfort and safety. Instead, it appears that the reenactment narrative is so disorganizing that it is incompletely processed as an overwhelming trauma by proxy, a vicarious "phantom" dying that was not directly experienced.

- The narrative of *resurrection* is a stabilizing narrative for the compulsive care-seeker with low tolerance for distress with separation and the resultant sense of self-disintegration. Death in this instance was the primary trauma, and resurrection retold is therefore alluring and comforting.
- The narrative of *reenactment* is an oppressive narrative for the intense caregiver who cannot tolerate the distress of trauma combined with failed obligation in maintaining the integrity and safety of the deceased who died alone and violently. Dying in this instance was the primary trauma, and reenactment retold is binding and remorseful.

These fixations may occur in combination because their attachment determinants (caregiving and care-seeking vulnerabilities) are not discontinuous. The representations, roles, actions, and goals of the survivor in either resurrection or reenactment fixation tend to be narrow and extreme.

It is important to note that there are conditions under which violent dying is presumably less traumatic and abhorrent. For instance, after a long interval of mental or physical despair, the bereaved and deceased may have anticipated dying as a desperate but positive act, and suicide (particularly elective suicide, where the family has a role in the dying story) may be followed by a mixture of sorrow for the deceased, and relief and release from their suffering. Under divergent conditions of persistent and chronic intra-family abuse and/or neglect there may be so little residual attachment (in either caregiving or care-receiving) between the bereaved and the abusive figure who died violently that his or her dying may elicit little distress.

A DYNAMIC MODEL OF REENACTMENT FIXATION AND COMPLICATED GRIEF

The effects of violent dying on complicated grief (reenactment images, flashbacks, recurring dreams accompanied by autonomic arousal, and avoidance) can be subsumed under a separate co-occurring diagnosis of posttraumatic stress disorder. Alternatively, the modeling of violent dying and grief might fit more parsimoniously within the capacious framework of the Dual Process Model (DPM) of complicated grief (Stroebe & Schut, 2010). Under the DPM framework, violent dying would be accessory to the loss-orientated referent as a reciprocal and oscillating dynamic represented in the following diagram of the DPM:

The Dual Process Model of Bereavement:
In the Context of Violent Dying

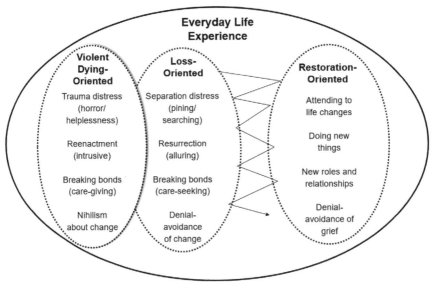

Within this revised DPM framework, when the trauma distress of violent dying reenactment is disinhibited, the violent dying orientation may predominate over the loss orientation and interfere with the loss/restoration dynamic. It is difficult to process the more vulnerable ruminations of loss when the mind is in a state of helpless entrapment, struggling to save and survive the intrusive onslaught of nihilistic violence. "Grief work," the dynamic oscillation between loss and restoration, might be hindered by the possessive demands of the reenactment intrusion and its dynamic residuals.

Interventions for complicated grief after violent dying

Studies of complicated grief include mixed samples of deaths from natural and violent dying (Boelen, 2007; Shear, Frank, Patrick, & Reynolds, 2005) and found no significant differences between violent and natural dying subjects on measures of trauma, grief, or discrepancies noted in treatment effects. Boelen recognized a dynamic differential in the avoidance of reenactment imagery after violent dying and focused imaginary exposure more intently on that imagery, but this is referenced in a footnote without a more detailed description. It is noteworthy that every intervention study cites frequencies of violent dying higher than predicted from its baseline frequency of 7%, suggesting a positive association of complicated grief and violent dying in intervention sampling (Cleiren, 1991; Rynearson, Schut, & Stroebe, 2012).

Presumably, a more specific intervention for complicated grief after violent dying might be indicated for subjects presenting with overwhelming reenactment fixations undetected or unelaborated by standardized empirical measures. A cascade of questions regarding reenactment fixations necessarily follows:

- Are there any standardized measures of narrative fixations?
- What is the normal frequency of reenactment fixations after natural or violent dying?
- Are there demographic, developmental, and relationship risk factors for the presence of intense reenactment fixations?
- Are specific types of violent dying associated with more intense and/or specific fixations?

Valid answers to these questions await development of specific measures of resurrection and reenactment responses, as well as traits of intense caregiving and care-receiving, including serial monitoring of their patterns, vectors, and combinations following natural and violent dying in clinical and community-based samples (Rynearson, 2016).

There are five manualized, time-limited, focused interventions specifically designed for violent dying. Three (Layne et al., 2009; Salloum, 2008; Cohen, Mannarino, & Staron, 2006) are designed for children and adolescent outpatients and two (Rynearson, Correa, Favell, Saindon, & Prigerson, 2006; Rynearson & Salloum, 2011; Murphy 1996, 2008) for adults. Unfortunately, there is no duplication of measures across studies to allow cross-comparison. Empirical pilot studies document significant decrease of trauma and grief distress in each of these intervention studies, but only two (Layne's study of Bosnian youth with traumatic grief and Murphy's community-based study of parents) include a control group and follow-up measures that document therapeutic effectiveness (Layne et al., 2009; Murphy, 1996).

Four of the interventions applied combined techniques from cognitive-behavioral therapy (CBT) and narrative therapy. CBT principles included structured, time-limited agendas (10 to 12 individual or group sessions); relationship-based collaboration; clarification of connections between thoughts, feelings, and behaviors;

affirmative guidance; relaxation exercises; modeling; and teaching techniques of imaginative exposure. Strategies based on narrative therapy encouraged the retelling of the living and dying story of the deceased with a restorative goal of creating a more plausible and coherent retelling of the narrative imagery of reenactment, promoting alternative outcomes and a transcendent perspective.

Unlike the other interventions, the support group designed by Murphy included problem-focused and emotion-focused support without sessions of direct exposure and retelling of the traumatic dying reenactment, though participants presumably shared their narratives of the living and dying of the deceased spontaneously during the support group.

None of these manualized interventions cite a specific, corrective "mechanism," and that is presumably because the explanation of treatment effects is non-specific. Interventions are successful because various intervention agendas are based upon the common principles of stress moderation, reconstructive exposure, and meaningful reengagement that follow a common ordinal phasing of therapeutic focus basic to time-limited trauma or grief treatments with at least three prevailing and phased goals:

> (1) First the moderation of distress (through a confiding relationship, a safe setting, psycho-education, and stress reduction strategies) that fosters mastery of personal safety and autonomy.
>
> (2) Then exposure and reconstructive processing of the dying and grieving narrative through an active procedure of "reliving" the narrative fixation (through imaginary verbal and non-verbal retelling) fostering coherence and motivation for reengagement by revising the teller's role (identity) within the narrative.
>
> (3) Finally, meaningful reengagement with valued, vital activities and relationships within the family and community in an altered identity that honors the transformation.

Treatment implications of reenactment fixations

When reenactment imagery is prominent and sustained (see DPM diagram), moderating trauma distress through techniques of resilience reinforcement (somatic relaxation and guided imagery) presumably takes priority before reenactment exposure. Once the patient has reestablished skills of self-calming and self-differentiation, alternative modes of exposure to the violent dying narrative are available to reinforce the sense of self-control of the imagery (writing, drawing, speaking, reading newspaper accounts, audio tapes, 911 tapes, or viewing TV reports) to be retold and revised with therapist and/or group. While exposure appears to be a significant therapeutic variable, its purpose is reconstructive rather than extirpative. When treating a patient traumatized by rape or other assault, the familiar model of graded exposure followed by extinction of the traumatic memory is appropriate, but after the violent dying of a loved one the dynamic is more complex. There is no resurrection narrative of another after an assault because no one has died. After violent dying the narratives of reenactment and resurrection of the deceased are co-existent and imbalanced. The early goal of exposure after violent dying is to include the living image of the deceased as vibrant and integral. Therapeutic pressure to "say goodbye" or "let go" of the imagery of the deceased before restoration might be resisted, misinterpreted by the patient as abandonment of their obligation to mend the suffering through compulsive caregiving of the deceased. The violated image of the deceased after violent dying presumably needs psychological repair and restoration before being released and mourned. Introducing the voice of the deceased through an imaginary conversation can serve as a reparative source of stability and meaning. The projected "presence" of the deceased may be actively enlisted during the intervention so the therapy frame becomes triadic as well as dyadic. The voice of the deceased may soften remorse and encourage self-forgiveness and detachment.

The demand for retaliation and retribution is particularly intense when the dying was premeditated (such as homicide or terrorism) or caused by gross negligence (such as drunk driving or industrial poisoning). Retaliation, most frequently observed in adolescent and adult males after homicide or terrorism, serves a reciprocal function shared by the surrounding community as vicarious retribution for the victimization and dishonor of the deceased. The demand for "consequences" after violent dying offers a compensatory role of potency for those attached to the victim, whose life is perceived as disregarded and disrespected. It is rare that someone bent on retaliation presents to a mental health clinician because relief of distress is viewed as contingent on an external counteraction, i.e., "I know what to do to feel better — I need to get even." However, this strident demand for retaliation and retribution may serve as an "acting out" or displacement of unacknowledged conflict associated with submission and impaired self-respect.

CLINICAL ILLUSTRATION

Dorothy, the mother of Mary, whose violent dying was briefly described at the beginning of this chapter, had begun treatment 6 months after Mary's rape and murder and was referred to our center by her psychiatrist. Dorothy's presenting complaints (despondency, insomnia, panic attacks, and inability to return to work as a nurse or enjoy her role as wife and mother) had been diagnosed as major depressive disorder and panic disorder, complicating her grief. These disorders were treated by the referring psychiatrist with medications (a selective serotonin reuptake inhibitor and a minor tranquilizer), combined with brief supportive visits every two weeks. The medications controlled her panic attacks, but after 4 months of negligible improvement in her grief, her husband insisted on a second opinion. He was having a difficult time tolerating her obsessive memorializing of their daughter and her daily flashbacks and nightmares of the dying.

At the beginning of the first session at our center, she could not stop herself from crying as she began to talk about her daughter's dying and stated, "I don't want to talk about it. It's all I think about and it just makes me feel worse to tell." This disinhibition had been noted by her referring psychiatrist, and listening and empathizing with her reenactment retelling had not been helpful.

I told her we needed to talk about her daughter's living before we talked about her dying. At my urging, she retrieved pictures from her purse and grew more animated as the pictures passed between us. Dorothy was convinced that her Mary's spirit was in heaven awaiting a reunion. I reflected how reassuring it must be to know that her daughter was in a safe place that promised a continuing connection.

I asked if she continued to have conversations with her daughter. She replied, "Yes, I talk to her every day."

I asked if she could imagine a two-way conversation. How would Mary feel about her seeing me as a therapist, and what suggestions would she give us to help? Dorothy thought about it and then said, "She would want me to see you and to tell me to stop missing her so much and stop me from blaming myself." (Note: I ask about spiritual beliefs and continuing communication with the deceased during an assessment of a highly-traumatized patient because it often evokes a therapeutic conversation that includes the voice of the deceased as a helpful projected presence. Establishing a triadic alliance between therapist, patient, and the deceased can be enriching and stabilizing).

Dorothy agreed with Mary's advice, and we ended that first session with resilience reinforcement, building her skills in deep breathing, muscle relaxation, and guided imagery. She selected a comforting image of sitting beside a mountain stream. We avoided directly talking about her reenactment flashbacks during the assessment, and I suggested that she actively divert her mind when the flashbacks recurred by concentrating on Mary's photo and hearing her say, "stop blaming yourself, Mom, I'm OK now."

She slowly discontinued her medications while attending weekly one-hour sessions during the next month. We strengthened her resilience by actively commemorating Mary's life, beginning with a survey of her baby album, her expertise in knitting (Dorothy proudly wore one of her sweaters), pictures of Mary's steady boyfriend, and discussion of her plans to attend nursing school. Gaining more confidence in her capacity to comfort herself with the exercises we practiced at the end of each session and by evoking Mary's reassuring presence and message of safety, Dorothy felt more detached from the daily flashbacks. But they did persist, so she agreed to join a closed group composed of survivors of violent death in a 10-session focused protocol. The intervention protocol followed a written agenda (Rynearson, 2016) of three phases: the first to reinforce resilience and moderate distress; the second to commemorate the life of the deceased, followed by exposure and revision of the reenactment narrative; the third to consolidate therapeutic changes, including a session with family and/or supportive friends and a termination session with a ritual farewell for the deceased.

The group support and reinforcement of her resilience during the first phase of the group strengthened her stability. However, the second phase was particularly helpful in transcending her self-blame for Mary's dying. This occurred during the presentation of her drawing of the reenactment imagery when her feelings of remorse were particularly intense. The image of Mary's dying was represented as a blackened circle with Mary's spirit as a winged angel transcending the death scene. She could not allow herself to "see" the actual events of torture and murder, and we did not encourage its explicit representation. Somehow, she had to make the dying "unhappen." The therapist noted that her drawing did not include her own presence and asked where she would introduce herself. She placed herself at the side of her daughter in the dark circle, sacrificing herself to the torture and murder.

The therapist invited Mary's voice into that revised image, asking how she would feel about her mother dying in her place. Mary protested, saying her mother's sacrifice would not have stopped the killing because both would have been murdered together. She reminded her mother that her father and two siblings needed her strength and attention. With the empathic reinforcement of several mothers in the group, Dorothy began to acknowledge that their children, including Mary, would not want them to continue suffering. The group members' voices joined Mary's in surrendering their collective burden of remorse as allies identified with the mutual dilemma of failed caregiving.

Dorothy's husband attended a group session during the third phase with family members and friends to encourage their collaboration in treatment. He was encouraged by her progress and at the end of the session requested a consultation. During the meeting, he was able to tearfully admit the sorrow and helplessness he had consciously suppressed while over-determined to "be strong" for his wife and surviving children and to obtain justice and retaliation for his murdered daughter. By allowing himself to openly mourn Mary's loss, he felt more empathic and tolerant of the grief work that he and Dorothy needed to share together.

At the completion of the group, the flashbacks of Mary's dying were now counterbalanced by memories and images of her enlivened and supportive "presence". In a final termination session, as each member constructed a farewell message to the group and one another, Dorothy included Mary's voice in a written message that read, "Thanks for helping my mom. She's doing a lot better and now she needs to get back to work and living for herself."

A year after her treatment began, Mary's mother reported that the flashbacks and dreams of her daughter's dying were infrequent since the intervention. She could now think of Mary without being overwhelmed with reenactment imagery and felt that returning to her work as a nurse and being present for the birth of her first grandson were of equal importance in her restoration.

Complicated grief after violent dying is a "reactive" experience as well as a syndrome or disorder. The dying and death of someone emotionally valued evokes vibrant stories of their living and dying as narrative remembrances. Highly subjective, intertwined, and multifarious grief narratives are difficult to quantify or measure. Measurements of distress responses and diagnostic criteria of complicated grief are informative, but the treating clinician remains anchored in sharing and revising the private nexus of intense and prolonged narratives of dying and death through a process of restorative retelling.

Edward K. Rynearson, MD, is a semi-retired clinical psychiatrist from Seattle, WA, where he founded the section of psychiatry at Virginia Mason. In addition to full-time clinical practice, he has served on the clinical faculty of the University of Washington as a clinical professor of psychiatry. For over 30 years, Dr. Rynearson has maintained a clinical and research focus on the effects of violent death on family members published in clinical papers, book chapters, and a book entitled Retelling Violent Death. *Since his retirement from full-time practice, he has given numerous national and international trainings on the management of the clinical effects of violent death and, with grant support, has founded a non-profit organization (the Violent Death Bereavement Society, www.vdbs.org) to establish an informative network for service providers, teachers, and researchers of violent death.*

References

Boelen, P. A. (2007) Treatment of complicated grief: Comparison between cognitive behaviour therapy and supportive counselling. *Journal of Counselling and Clinical Psychology,* 277-84.

Cleiren, M. (1991). *Adaptation to bereavement.* University of Leiden, NL: DSWO Press.

Cohen, J. A., Mannarino, A. P., & Staron, V. (2006). A pilot study for modified cognitive-behavioral therapy for childhood traumatic grief. *Journal of the Academy of Child and Adolescent Psychiatry, 45,* 1465-1473.

Currier, J., Holland, J., & Neimeyer, R. (2006). Sense-making, grief, and the experience of violent loss: Toward a mediational model. *Death Studies, 30,* 403-428.

Flor, H., Elbert, T., Knecht, S., Wienbruch, C., Pantev, C., Birbaumer, N., & Taub, E. (1995). Phantom-limb pain as a perceptual correlate of cortical reorganization following arm amputation. *Nature, 375,* 482–484.

Gundel, H., O'Connor, M. F., Littrell, L., Fort, C., & Lane, R. D. (2003). Functional neuroanatomy of grief: An fMRI Study. *American Journal of Psychiatry, 160,* 1946–1953. 10.1176/appi.ajp.160.11.1946

Jacobs, S. (1999). *Traumatic Grief: Diagnosis, Treatment and Prevention.* Philadelphia, PA: Taylor & Francis.

Layne, C. M., Saltzman, W. R., Poppleton, L., Burlingame, G. M., Pasalic, A., Durakovic, E.,...Pynoos, R. S. (2009). Effectiveness of a school-based psychotherapy for war-exposed adolescents: A randomized controlled trial. *Journal of the Academy of Child and Adolescent Psychiatry, 47,* 1048-1062.

Murphy, S. (1996). Parent bereavement stress and preventive intervention following the violent deaths of adolescent or young adult children. *Death Studies, 2,* 441-452.

Murphy, S. (2008). The loss of a child: Sudden death and extended illness perspectives. In M. Stroebe, R. O. Hansson, H. Schut, & W. Stroebe (Eds.), *Handbook of bereavement research and practice: Advances in theory and intervention* (pp. 375-395). Washington, DC: APA.

Rynearson, E. K. (2001). *Retelling violent death.* New York, NY: Brunner-Routledge.

Rynearson, E. K. (2016). Grief training, consultation and mental health services. Retrieved January 9, 2017, from Violent death bereavement society (VDBS), http://www.vdbs.org/

Rynearson, E. K., Correa, F., Favell, J., Saindon, C. & Prigerson, H. (2006). Restorative retelling after violent dying. In E. K. Rynearson (Ed.), *Violent dying: Resilience and intervention beyond the crisis* (pp. 195-216). New York, NY: Taylor and Francis.

Rynearson, E. K. & Salloum, A. (2011). Restorative retelling: Revising the narrative of violent death. In R. Neimeyer (Ed.), *Grief and Bereavement in Contemporary Society* (pages 177-188). New York, NY: Routledge.

Rynearson, E. K., Schut, H., & Stroebe, M. (2012). Complicated grief after violent death: Identification and intervention. In M. Stroebe, H. Schut, and J. Van den Bout (Eds.), *Complicated Grief* (pages 278-292). New York, NY: Routledge.

Rynearson, E. K. (2016). Treating the narrative fixations of grief. *Grief Matters, 19*(1), 14-17.

Salloum, A. (2008). Group therapy for children experiencing grief and trauma due to homicide and violence: A pilot study. *Research and Social Work Practice, 18*, 198-211.

Shear, K., Frank, E., Patrick, H., & Reynolds, C. (2005). Treatment of Complicated Grief: A randomized controlled trial. *Journal of the American Medical Association, (293)*21, 2601-2608.

Stroebe, M. S., & Schut, H. (2010). The Dual Process Model of coping with bereavement: A decade on. *OMEGA—Journal of Death and Dying, 61*, 273-289.

CHAPTER 9

Recognizing and Treating Complicated Grief

M. Katherine Shear

Complicated grief is a condition in which adaptation to loss is derailed and acute grief persists for an inordinate period of time. Our clinical research team began work more than 20 years ago to understand and treat bereaved people who sought professional help because of prolonged intense grief that was interfering with their lives. To do so we drew upon research findings by behavioral scientists that are valid across cultures. Though we recognized that each person grieves in his or her own way, we learned there were also commonalities in bereavement, grief, and adaptation to loss that could serve as a framework to guide therapeutic assessment and intervention. Our work has been rewarded by clear demonstration of the accuracy of our assessment methods (Bui et al., 2015; Prigerson et al., 1995) and beneficial effects of our 16-session complicated grief treatment (CGT) intervention (Shear, Frank, Houck, & Reynolds, 2005; Shear et al., 2014, 2016). The strong evidence for both the validity of identifying the syndrome we call complicated grief and for the effectiveness of CGT is important but does not mean this is the only way to think about, or to work with, bereaved people. Patients will benefit most if clinicians are as informed as possible about different models, principles, and procedures for intervention and strive to personalize their treatment of any given individual. It is in this spirit that we share with readers our approach to assessment and treatment of complicated grief. We describe who we treat, what we do, and how we do it.

SETTING THE STAGE IN THE GRIEF THERAPY CONSULTING ROOM

Our clinical research team focuses attention on the nature of the therapeutic alliance in optimizing both assessment and treatment procedures. We believe therapists need to approach grief therapy with an organizing framework in mind but without expectations about what a client should be feeling, thinking, or doing. Many grief therapists come to the field after suffering their own intense grief; they intuitively know how important it is to recognize that everyone grieves in their own way, and that there is no prescription for how to adapt to a painful loss. Other therapists who work with the grieving may need to learn this important principle.

The assessment and treatment alliance in CGT follows five basic principles that resemble the way that Sherpa guides in the Himalayas work to assist climbers. The five principles of a Sherpa-like Companionship Alliance are to:

- understand the experience of loss and grief;
- help design pathways to adaptation;
- recognize obstacles to adaptation to the loss (grief complications);
- have access to supplies of information, activities, and resources; and
- contribute only when there is a specific reason to do so.

A fundamental principle of this work is the need to understand the experience of loss and grief. We supply CGT therapists with a model that is rooted in attachment theory and related research findings about close human relationships. This foundation explains commonalities in grief and provides a map for designing pathways to adaptation and monitoring progress in doing so. This model further helps explain how and what can stand in the way of the progress of adaptation, creating the syndrome of complicated grief. We further provide a 16-session intervention model that offers patients encouragement, information, activities, and a range of resources that can be used to resolve grief complications and facilitate the progress of adaptation. Importantly, we strongly advocate that therapists attend to their own responses to loss and grief and ensure that they focus on supporting the patient's natural adaptive capacity, contributing their own ideas only when necessary.

GRIEF FRAMEWORK

Attachment theory and relationships

Humans are social beings, and our close relationships are a biological as well as a psychological necessity. Scientists have been surprised at how pervasively our loved ones influence us, even in ways that we don't consciously realize. This influence occurs through their physical presence and also because they are mapped in our brain memory systems. We use memories of loved ones in our everyday life in a myriad of ways, many of which are out of our awareness. Thinking about a loved one, even when those thoughts are triggered in a way that we don't know is happening, can affect how we regulate our attention, the degree of curiosity we feel, how we make decisions, our reaction time, distractibility, and memory functioning, just to name a few. Thoughts or images of someone we love can affect our physical functioning, including hormone levels, cardiovascular activity, and immune function. Again, this can occur when someone we care about is present, when we focus attention on thoughts of them when they are absent, and even when the thoughts or images of a loved one are activated out of our awareness. We all know that loved ones are important, but few people fully appreciate the depth and breadth to which this is true. Knowing how pervasively they influence us can help us understand why their loss can be so devastating.

Caregiving and exploration

Biological motivational systems for caregiving and exploration are linked to attachment, such that losing a loved one is affected by these systems as well. As adults, we provide, as well as receive, care. Being an effective caregiver matters a lot to most of us and contributes importantly to our sense of identity and feelings of wellbeing. A bereaved person often has feelings that she has failed to provide a safe haven for the deceased person, even with the understanding that this is probably not true. If the bereaved person gets caught up in ruminating over feelings of failure as a caregiver, this undermines a sense of self-efficacy and lowers mood. The inability to resolve the tendency to second-guess something about the circumstances of the death interrupts restorative processes and is a common way grief can become complicated.

Another biological system motivates us to explore the world and learn new things, to perform and achieve. The exploratory system orients us to want to be our own person and to want to meet challenges. One of the things we get (and give) in our close relationships is someone who shares our joy in the fulfillment that comes from activities that are genuinely interesting and satisfying. When our loved ones are alive and our relationship with them is strong, caregiving and exploration are also optimized. When they die, all of these systems are affected. In short, it's like an earthquake has shaken the foundation of our lives.

Loss and grief

Loss of a loved one is one of the most difficult events we experience in our lives. Grief is the natural instinctive response to loss, and its quality is different than anything else we experience, at least as adults. The difference is related to the pervasive influence that our loved ones have on a range of regulatory functions and sense of security. It is also connected to the impact of losing rewarding interactions and self-defining inputs we have grown to expect from our loved one. Our loved ones are deeply embedded in our lives and in our minds. They have a special place in our memories, motivations, and behavioral control systems. When someone very close to us dies, it affects us deeply, and its effects are permanent. Losing someone close changes us forever.

People respond instinctively to loss with grief, just as they respond instinctively to danger with fear. The intensity and pain usually subside, but people never stop missing someone they love or feeling sad they are gone. The sorrow does get more muted and, importantly, even in the presence of this sorrow, most people find a way to restore their sense of self, their feelings of competence, and their interest in activities that are genuinely interesting and valued.

Acute grief

In the beginning, grief is almost always very painful. Losing someone close feels like there is a hole in the fabric of our lives that nothing can ever repair. Another metaphor is that it feels like we are lost at sea: the anchor has been cut, storm clouds are on the horizon, and there is no compass or chart to guide us. All we can do is try to stay afloat and trust that forces out of our control will take us someplace where we can navigate again. The more importance the person who died had in our lives, the more rewarding the relationship, then the more intense are these feelings. Typical symptoms of acute grief include strong feelings of yearning, longing, sadness, and a feeling of disbelief or difficulty comprehending the reality of the death. There are frequent preoccupying thoughts and images of the person who died and difficulty caring about anything else. Often bereaved people feel confused about who they are or what matters to them after a loved one dies.

There may also be feelings of remorse or even pangs of guilt, focused on having let the deceased person down in some way. One aspect of acute grief is related to a sense of caregiving failure. When a loved one dies, the caregiving system automatically generates self-accusatory thoughts: "We weren't vigilant enough. We dropped the ball. We failed to act when we should have. It was our job to take care of this person and we failed." People usually have these thoughts even when their rational mind knows perfectly well that what happened was not their fault. It's very difficult to have self-blaming thoughts when already upset by loss, and it can be surprisingly difficult to resolve them, but not impossible. In fact, most people find a way to do it.

Adaptation to loss

When someone we love dies, we have to assimilate information about the finality of the death and its meaning so that our motivational and behavioral control processes can access this information. We need to revise our memories of them so that expectations generated from our memory systems are not unrealistic. We must reorganize our ways of defining ourselves to incorporate the information about our loved one's death in order to begin to envision and plan our own future differently. These processes take time. It is helpful to trust in the instinctive process that guides adaptation, but people often worry instead that there is something wrong with them or with what they are feeling. They are often inclined to try to avoid painful reminders of their loss, though repeated confrontation with these reminders is a part of the way we gradually adapt to the emotionally painful reality that our loved one is gone.

Our minds move naturally back and forth between paying attention to the painful reality and then setting it aside. We observe and reflect on our new situation from the perspective of what we have lost and from the perspective of what remains. Out of these two perspectives we gradually construct new possibilities. We each do this in our own way, adjusting the period of confrontation and respite to our own rhythm.

What is important is that we engage in this process and not avoid it. An important component is to practice self-compassion during this period of adaptation.

Other people are important in the process of adapting to a loss; in general, we don't grieve well alone. Loss of a loved one presents us with a challenging assortment of emotional and practical problems. Companions can help us by providing solace and assistance in problem-solving if we let them, as well as serve as loving reminders that the present and future can still hold possibilities for happiness. Positive emotions can also help if we allow ourselves to have those, even for short periods of time. Positive emotions nourish our minds like healthy food nourishes our bodies. By balancing confrontation with pain and respite, sharing and companionship with solitude, painful emotions with pleasurable ones, and attention to the past with a focus on the future, we can move forward in our own lives after loss. As we adapt to the loss, grief is gradually reshaped.

Integrated grief

Over time we usually repair the rift in our lives. We leave the open sea and once again find a safe harbor. Emotional pain subsides, and we feel less pressure to focus on thoughts and memories of the person who died and become more interested in our own lives and futures. Grief is not over, but its intensity, frequency, and duration diminish and it becomes integrated into our ongoing life. We start to feel whole again and regain our confidence. Of course, this doesn't mean we stop caring about our loved one who died or stop wishing we could have them back. Rather, we come to understand the multifaceted reality of the death and figure out a way forward in a world infused with their absence. Another way to visualize it is that we move a loved one from preoccupying our mind to residing peacefully in our heart. Humans have the capacity to integrate grief instinctively; yet, for a person with complicated grief, it can seem like that is not possible.

DESCRIBING THE SYNDROME OF COMPLICATED GRIEF

Complicated grief is the condition that results when adaptation to loss is stalled or halted by grief complications in the form of thoughts, feelings, or actions. People with complicated grief are caught up in something that troubles them about the death or its consequences. They can't seem to shake the idea that they, someone else, or even the larger world, failed in an unforgivable way. Their thoughts are focused on imagining how things might have been different. They often feel a need to deprive or punish themselves or others for the failure or because it seems unfair to enjoy life when the person who died can no longer do so. They resist the idea that life can be meaningful without their loved one. The present is filled with pain, and the future looks empty and dark; their only respite is in the past.

People struggling with complicated grief see no possibility of happiness in the present or future, instead recalling how wonderful things were when their loved one was present. They long to have the deceased person back and feel bitter and angry that the person is gone. They might immerse themselves in thoughts of the past in a way that excludes the loss. They may try not to think about the fact that their loved one is gone; usually, this means avoiding reminders. Of course, reminders of our loved ones are ubiquitous, so trying to avoid them is inevitably futile. As a result, people with complicated grief spend a lot of energy trying to figure out how to do everything differently in their lives in order to avoid reminders, only to find that this is a discouraging task that is probably impossible to achieve. The last thing on their mind is making peace with the reality of the death. Yet, paradoxically, the route to restoration of a meaningful life is by this road not taken. The places they are trying so hard to avoid visiting or even seeing are the very places they need to inhabit. The more they try to escape from the painful reality, the more intense and insistent acute grief becomes. Naturally this usually leads to redoubling of the effort to escape.

A simple way of recognizing complicated grief

The specific thoughts, feelings, and behaviors that pervade the lives of people with complicated grief are as varied as the people themselves and their differing loss experiences. However, there are a few simple reliable ways to recognize people who are struggling in this way. The 19-item Inventory of Complicated Grief (ICG) is an excellent screening tool (Prigerson et al., 1995). In both clinical and community-based studies, a score of 30 on this instrument is highly likely to be associated with complicated grief. People who score between 20-30 are also at some elevated risk for complicated grief. While the ICG has been revised in recent years, we believe the original instrument is the simplest and most effective screening tool. Use of the ICG can be supplemented by a clinical interview to identify evidence of persisting acute grief, complicating features like those described above, and evidence that grief is interfering in the bereaved person's life.

The most current American Psychiatric Association (APA) *Diagnostic and Statistical Manual* (5th ed.; *DSM-5*; 2013) has included a diagnosis of persistent complex bereavement disorder as a form of adjustment disorder with specific criteria included in Section III, "Conditions in Need of Further Study." Three studies of the diagnostic criteria are now available. One is a replication of previously reported findings (Maciejewski, Maercker, Boelen, & Prigerson, 2016); one is in a community-based sample comprised of primarily violent death bereavement (Cozza et al., 2016); and the third is in a clinical sample (Mauro et al., 2016). All three show that criteria our group proposed in 2011 (Shear et al., 2011) are the only one of the three proposed criteria sets with acceptable sensitivity to complicated grief.

Proposed Diagnostic Criteria for Complicated Grief

A. The person experienced the death of a loved one at least 6 months ago.

B. At least one of the following symptoms of persistent intense grief has been present for a period longer than is expected by others in the person's social or cultural environment:

1) Persistent intense yearning or longing for the person who died;

2) Frequent intense feelings of loneliness or that life is empty or meaningless without the person who died;

3) Recurrent thought that it is unfair or meaningless to have to live when the person they love died, or a recurrent urge to die in order to find or to join the deceased, or because life seems unbearable without this person;

4) Frequent preoccupying or intrusive thoughts about the person who died (e.g., thoughts or images of the person) that are so frequent that they intrude on usual activities or interfere with functioning.

C. At least two of the following symptoms are present for at least a month:

1) Frequent troubling rumination about circumstances or consequences of the death (e.g., concerns about how or why the person died, thoughts that the bereaved person can't manage without their loved one, feeling of having let the deceased person down, etc.);

2) Recurrent feeling of disbelief or inability to accept the death (e.g., the person feels that they can't believe/accept that their loved one is really gone);

3) Recurrent feelings of anger or bitterness related to the death;

4) Persistent feeling of being shocked, stunned, dazed, or emotionally numb since the death;

5) Persistent difficulty trusting or caring about other people, or feeling intensely envious of people who haven't experienced a similar loss;

6) Frequently experiencing pain or other symptoms that the deceased person had, or hearing the voice of or seeing the deceased person;

7) Experiencing intense emotional or physiological reactivity to memories of the person who died or to reminders of the loss;

8) Change in behavior due to excessive avoidance (e.g., refraining from going places, doing things, or having contact with things that are reminders of the loss); or excessive proximity-seeking (e.g., feeling drawn to reminders of the person such as wanting to see, touch, hear or smell things to feel close to the person who died).

Criteria for both prolonged grief disorder and persistent complex bereavement disorder fail to identify 30% to 40% of people with clear evidence of complicated grief symptoms and substantial impairment in functioning (Cozza et al., 2016; Mauro et al., 2016). A brief semi-structured clinical interview is available through the Center for Complicated Grief (https://complicatedgrief.columbia.edu/).

INTRODUCING COMPLICATED GRIEF TREATMENT (CGT): TREKKING THE RUGGED TERRAIN

Complicated Grief Treatment (CGT) is a 16-session intervention that uses seven core components administered in four phases.

Seven Core Components of CGT	Four phases of CGT
1. Lay of the land	1. Getting started
2. Self-regulation	2. Core revisiting sequence
3. Aspirational goals	3. Midcourse review
4. Rebuilding connection	4. Closing sequence
5. Revisiting the story of the death	
6. Revisiting the world	
7. Memories and continuing bonds	

The sessions are fairly brief. Clinicians can think of them as oriented toward coaching the patient to monitor, realign, and commit to a plan for activities they will do between the sessions. The treatment relies on this interval work. Most complicated grief patients have been working hard to keep grief out of their lives; the treatment helps people accept grief into their lives and encourages companionship in doing so. Interval work has a considerable impact on the ability to accomplish these goals. It may be that adaptation is successful only when we allow grief to infuse our everyday lives. We make an assumption that loss activates a psychological immune system that can guide people through an innate adaptation process if they do not get in their own way.

Therapists demonstrate leadership by planning, structuring, and having confidence in the process. We want the patient to feel warmly welcomed and appreciative of this leadership. CGT sessions begin by welcoming the patient warmly and getting agreement to set an agenda. During most of the sessions, the patient is doing a lot of interval work through grief monitoring, listening to revisiting tapes, or working on situational revisiting, Memories Forms, and personal aspirational goals. The standard agenda devotes about half of the office time to a loss-focused activity and the other half to a restoration focus. Sessions end with check-in, feedback, and plans for the upcoming week.

The seven core components

The overall objective of complicated grief treatment is to identify and resolve grief complications and to facilitate the natural adaptive process. Adaptation entails accepting the reality of the loss, including its finality and consequences; revising the internalized working model of the deceased person to create a sense of the continuing bond with this person; and fostering the capacity to reenvision a future with the promise of joy and satisfaction in a new normal world infused with the absence of the person who died. The seven core components are designed to help achieve these goals. They are introduced sequentially and track through multiple sessions and phases of the treatment.

Component 1: Lay of the land

This first component entails collecting and providing information to lay the groundwork for the treatment. Central to this effort is the ability to create a collaborative, supportive environment for people to explore intense emotions, take risks, and make important changes in their lives. One way to think about people with complicated grief is that they are unwilling or unable to make the decision to live their lives without the person who died. They have most likely been told by others, quite directly and not without frustration, "You have been grieving long enough. It's time to move on." This situation bears some resemblance to what happens to people with substance use disorders. The great insight from the technique of Motivational Interviewing (MI) is that when people with alcohol abuse disorders are told all the reasons to stop drinking, the ambivalence is shifted to the side of continuing to drink (Miller & Rollnick, 1991). Something similar happens with people coping with complicated grief; the more they are told to move on, the more they are convinced they cannot.

An important job for the CGT therapist is to create an atmosphere conducive to resolving this ambivalence. Moreover, in order to resolve it, the patient must confront some of the most painful emotions he has ever felt. It is critical that the therapist be skilled in developing a collaborative relationship, displaying empathy without intrusion, and in practicing reflective listening. The therapist needs to elicit and understand the patient's point of view without seeking to change it. In grief treatment, this means that the therapist does not present the counter-argument to irrational or dysfunctional thoughts, especially those related to caregiver self-blame or anger, or to ideas of being unable to manage or enjoy life without the loved one in it. The therapist needs to understand these ideas as natural products of the attachment and caregiving system. Instead of challenging these thoughts, the therapist accepts this perspective and possibly supports it.

For example, a mother whose son died by suicide was furious when the law enforcement officer confiscated the suicide note. She continued to ruminate on this incident for many years before seeking treatment. In discussing this, her therapist said she was not surprised at the intensity of the emotions, as she had been a deeply committed mother to her son. Her urge to protect his most private document was completely understandable. The patient thought for a minute and said that she thought a mother lion could not have been more fierce than she, and the therapist agreed. The patient then began to talk about different ways she had taken very good care of her son. This acknowledgment was an important step in working to accept the loss.

Many people with complicated grief struggle with trying to understand what led to the death. They become focused on whose fault it was and on how it could have been stopped. It may seem to the therapist, as it does to others in their lives, that this is fruitless rehashing of something that has no answer. Yet, the CGT therapist does not try to challenge these thoughts or try to convince the patient of alternative ways to see the situation. Instead, the therapist first empathizes with the fact that it is very hard to have these uncertainties that will never be fully resolved. However, this empathic statement is not made in order to accept the fact that the patient must forever more ruminate about these questions. It is a principle of MI that acceptance facilitates change. Acceptance, though, is simply the first step in a process by which the therapist can facilitate the patient's own resolution of this problem. The therapist uses MI strategies of developing discrepancy, rolling with resistance, and supporting self-efficacy to encourage the patient to reconsider her position.

The therapeutic stance in CGT is open and collaborative. The therapist has expertise in the area of complicated grief and other mental disorders, yet the attitude of the therapist is respectful and collaborative. The therapist can and should share her or his own opinion about various issues as they are discussed, identifying them as opinion and owning them. I usually tell people that I have an opinion and ask if they would like to hear it. When they say they want to hear,

I remind them that my opinion might not be right, but this is what I think, and (if I know) I tell them why.

Component 2: Self-regulation

Self-regulation refers to our capacity to set meaningful goals for ourselves and to regulate our thoughts, feelings, and behaviors in order to meet these goals. Acute grief undermines a person's capacity to engage in self-regulation. It is difficult to feel connected to, or to set goals for, the future, and it is difficult to regulate waves of intense painful emotions. In CGT, we seek to help a grieving person become an observer of his or her own thoughts, feelings, and behaviors and what triggers these. This process includes noticing both troubling thoughts and positive ones.

The CGT therapist works in a number of ways to encourage people to become self-observers. Two of the treatment procedures directly target this goal. The first is grief monitoring. The therapist introduces the grief monitoring diary at the end of the first treatment session, inviting the patient to take 5 to 10 minutes at the end of each day to record the highest and lowest level of her grief on a scale from 0 to 10, note the situations in which they occurred, and then record the average grief level for that day. Daily monitoring helps people see that their grief is not at a steady level, as they often believe it is, but rather that it fluctuates, usually in response to different situations.

For example, a patient reported that she had been having a reasonably good day, and suddenly she found herself missing her husband and feeling exceptionally sad. She was surprised by this until she noticed that the wave of grief was triggered when she went to a restaurant with her daughter and noticed all the happy couples at other tables. She had the thought that it was unfair that they had spouses and she did not. She told the therapist this was probably why she really didn't like going out to eat. She also noted in her diary a period of time when her grief level was very low. A friend had convinced her to get a puppy a few months earlier, hoping that it would help her snap out of her seemingly endless grief. On the day she recorded the low grief level, she had gone to the dog park for the first time and had been greatly amused watching her puppy play with the other dogs. She said she was pretty sure she actually laughed at some of his antics, something she could not remember doing in a very long time. The therapist told her that this was an important observation and a wonderful experience, and she wanted her to try to build on experiences like this. It is very important for bereaved people to take advantage of any genuine pleasure and happiness they feel.

Generally, as the treatment progresses, the bereaved person will experience more low grief levels. The therapist looks for genuine positive experiences, even small ones, indicating that low levels are not simply relief from the grief. These lower levels should increase over the second half of the treatment. When the therapist sees an indication of a positive experience in the monitoring or hears about it, we share enthusiasm for this. An example of this can be seen in Deborah's story.

Deborah's husband, Charles, died 4 years ago after a 6-month illness. Deborah had stopped going to dinner with her friends after his death. During CGT she did the revisiting exercise well and listened to the tape as instructed, and by session 6 she reported feeling "lighter." After session 7 she decided to accept a dinner invitation from her best friend. Her lowest grief rating for the day of the dinner was a 3, which was by far the lowest rating yet. Deborah seemed genuinely happy as she reported some of the details of the dinner party. She said everyone commented that they missed Charles. She found that she loved hearing that, and even though she was a little sad, she had a wonderful time. The therapist responded with enthusiasm, saying, "That is huge! I am so pleased to hear that you accepted an invitation. That is a pretty big move by itself, but that you genuinely enjoyed yourself is huge!" Deborah smiled broadly as she agreed, and they shared this positive experience.

The diary review can also focus on the overall pattern of grief. The therapist might comment on the pattern: "It looks like overall the average level of grief is a little lower this week" or "Overall, it looks like there are fewer really high levels and your low levels are occasionally a little lower, but the average level hasn't changed much yet." The therapist can encourage the patient to respond to this. Whichever way the therapist reviews the diary, we keep the opening segment of the session brief in order to allow sufficient time to cover the main content of the session.

Paradoxically, the therapist might occasionally use the diary to support a person's decision not to complete it. Here is one example of how we personalize this treatment. Pam was a 45-year-old woman grieving the loss of her husband 2 years earlier. She was generally a highly compliant and somewhat apologetic patient. However, in session 9 she told the therapist, with a touch of glee in her voice, that she missed one day of tape listening during the week and skipped doing her goal monitoring diary as well that day. She said that she had had a new, strange feeling that Saturday morning. She felt like she "just wanted to do what I felt like doing that day." Even though Pam was finding the diary helpful, she shared that she was getting tired of thinking about grief all the time, and had decided to give herself permission to take a day off. She recounted that she spent the day doing one pleasurable activity after the other, occasionally remembering fondly certain times with her husband. The therapist smiled as Pam reported this and told Pam that she thought she had made a great decision. The therapist realized that some of the activities Pam was referring to were things she had done before, like walking in the park or browsing in a knitting store, but the quality of her experience of these activities seemed to be different as she reported what she had done that Saturday. The therapist happily endorsed Pam's decision and told her it reflected important progress in being able to genuinely enjoy herself, while at the same time freely accessing warm memories.

In addition to the ongoing grief monitoring diary, we focus on self-observation and reflection in each of the other six components of the treatment as well.

Component 3: Aspirational goals

The fourth component of CGT focuses on understanding the bereaved person's intrinsic values and interests and using these to identify a long-term aspirational goal. Ideally, the therapist can encourage and support the person in a program designed to move forward in achieving this goal. Notably, this is not a treatment goal, in the sense that there is no effort to encourage or work with the patient to achieve this aspiration by the end of the treatment. Rather, we want to generate interest and enthusiasm for the future that can help the patient regain a sense of meaning and purpose in life and restore feelings of competence. To do this, we work to identify a personal life goal that is interesting and holds some promise of increasing joy, satisfaction, and pleasure in life.

The therapist begins personal goals work in the second session and this work is continued in each session thereafter. The therapist invites the patient to consider what she would want for herself, if her grief were at a manageable level. The procedure is modified from the MI approach to working on personalized treatment goals. The therapist helps the patient consider very concrete steps she can take, who can help her do this, what obstacles she might encounter, and how committed she is to the process.

Some people respond to the question of what they wish to achieve by immediately reporting several things they have been thinking about. For example, an older woman whose husband had driven her everywhere had been fantasizing about having a new car of her own. She had the brand and the color all picked out in her mind, even though she did not have a driver's license. Another patient said she had long held dreams of opening an antique store but had been unable to do so because of the intense caregiving needs of her mother; by the end of the treatment she had done just that.

Component 4: Rebuilding connection

One of the most difficult consequences of losing a loved one is the painful sense of disconnection the loss typically engenders. Acute grief is often associated with feeling disconnected from oneself, from other people we care about who are still alive, and from the world in general. In CGT, we work to help people become active and engaged in their lives and to reconnect to other people. The patient is encouraged to invite another person who is significant to him or her for a conjoint session during the first phase of the treatment, "Getting Started." We usually plan to do this in session 3, but we are flexible to accommodate the needs of both the person and their invited family member or friend. This procedure is done to begin the process of rebuilding a confiding relationship and to obtain additional information that the bereaved person may have neglected to provide. The purpose of the session is to elicit information about the relationship between the patient and the person who has died, and how the death may have affected this relationship.

The focus is on gathering honest care from the supportive friend or family member and on learning about what they think the patient is experiencing and why. We then provide information about love, loss, and grief and how we understand complicated grief and its treatment. This information is similar to psychoeducation provided to the patient in session 2. We discuss possible ways the patient thinks the important friend or family member might be helpful as they move through the treatment. Then, as the treatment progresses, the therapist looks for opportunities to encourage communication and activities with this person or someone else with whom the patient might begin to confide. The therapeutic goal is for the bereaved person to leave the treatment with at least one person in their life in whom she is comfortable confiding.

Component 5: Revisiting the story of the death

One of the important tasks of adaptation to loss is learning to accept the reality of the death. To do this we encourage the bereaved person to revisit the time when he first learned of his loved one's death. If the patient was present at the bedside or observed the death, this may be the time of the actual death. If not, we ask him to recall the phone call or other notification as the moment when he first learned of the death. CGT uses a modified version of prolonged exposure to encourage patients to confront the painful reality. This process entails asking the patient to close his eyes and visualize the moment when he first learned of the death. The patient continues to visualize what happened after that and tells this story to the therapist, who is also recording the story. This exercise is done for 10 minutes, during which time the therapist bears witness to the story and periodically asks the patient to report on his overall distress level using a scale of 1 to10. At the time of eliciting the levels, the therapist may add words of encouragement, such as, "You are doing a good job" or "You're doing fine; keep going," but otherwise does not comment.

At the end of 10 minutes, the therapist asks the patient to stop, open his eyes, and report an overall distress level. The therapist then encourages the patient to engage in self-observation and reflection on the story. The therapist again comments only to ask what the exercise was like and what he noticed or observed as he was telling the story. This self-reflection process is done for about 10 minutes, after which the therapist asks again for the distress level and then encourages the patient to set this story and the associated thoughts and feelings aside. The discussion moves to planning a rewarding activity that the patient can do to balance the pain of telling this story. At the end of the session, the patient is given the audio recording and asked to listen to the tape daily, if possible. The therapist makes plans to talk with the patient by phone after the first time, and assures the patient that he can call again if necessary, to assist the patient in doing the difficult revisiting exercises. Telephone sessions last about 10 to15 minutes and focus on the review of the revisiting exercise. One of the goals is to help the patient become a compassionate self-observer. Self-observations help clarify what has been bothering the patient, what is important to him, and where he might want to go next. For example, a patient who had taken good care of her elderly father as he died of cancer recalled that he had been grateful to her for her efforts. She had forgotten how he had thanked her, very emotionally, on the day he died. She recalled that she had felt close to him and had felt their love very strongly that afternoon, even though she knew he was dying. She shared that she felt lucky that they had had this time together. Yet, he had died later that night while she was not with him. Since his death, she had become preoccupied with guilty remorse. She also felt angry with the nurse who was there, thinking she could have saved him. The revisiting exercises were very difficult, but the memory of her loving interaction with her father was greatly reassuring.

Component 6: Revisiting the world

The main procedure we use for this component is situational revisiting. This is a series of exercises designed to remove restrictions in participating in activities, being with people, or going certain places. Avoidance of one's normal activities is often a last-ditch effort on the part of the patient with complicated grief to try to protect herself from the searing pain. Patients often provide vivid descriptions of their need to run away from reminders; yet reminders are everywhere, so this effort is often futile. Moreover, while respite from pain is certainly important, extensive avoidance restricts people from fully processing the loss and also from living a fully engaged and exuberant life. One patient said that she found herself thinking, "I can't go there because my mother liked to go there, and I can't go here because I went there with her." She went on to say, "Before you knew it, I wasn't going anywhere. I would just stay in my house and look out the window and feel a little angry because everyone else was just going about their business, like they didn't know that the world had lost someone wonderful."

The CGT therapist helps the patient identify situations he is avoiding. The distress associated with each situation is rated, as well as the degree to which the avoidance is restricting his life. Then the patient plans to repeatedly revisit a situation that is associated with moderate levels of distress and a high degree of restriction. This procedure serves several purposes. It reverses the process described by the patient above; instead of reducing the pain of her loss, avoidance only increases anxiety about feeling it. Additionally, revisiting difficult situations that are reminders of the finality of the loss is helpful in processing this information. The implicit memory system needs to learn not to expect the deceased person to appear in these familiar places. Situational revisiting also provides an opportunity to observe and work with the problematic thoughts and beliefs that are associated with the loss. Lastly, revisiting begins the process of reversing the restrictions the patient has placed on his life and opens opportunities for pleasure and satisfaction.

Component 7: Memories and continuing bonds

The final treatment component includes introduction of a series of Memories Forms and an invitation to the client to have an imaginal conversation with the person who died. The five sequential Memories Forms contain a series of questions about what the patient loved about the person who died, as well as what they did not love so much about the person. These questions are introduced after about three imaginal revisiting sessions and the patient completes one form a week for 5 weeks.

After the imaginal revisiting exercises have been completed, the patient is invited to have an imaginal conversation with the person who died. We invite the patient to close her eyes and imagine she is back at the time shortly after the death. The patient is invited to tell or ask the person anything, and then take the role of the person who died and answer. This exercise is a very powerful way for the patient to feel the sense of connection with her deceased loved one. The conversation can also be another opportunity to help the patient resolve any continuing troubling thoughts or feelings related to the death. (Details about this and other CGT procedures can be found at https://complicatedgrief. columbia.edu).

Treatment structure

Complicated Grief Treatment is administered in approximately 16 weekly therapy sessions that include planning for between-session continuity. Each session begins with a review of the time since the last visit and ends with a plan for the period until the next session. During the early period of revisiting exercises, the therapist is available for telephone consultation as much as is practically possible. Listening to the revisiting recording is usually the most difficult and most important of the between-session planned work. The therapist also actively works to help the patient identify other people who might help with difficult revisiting work and/or provide more general support.

The 16 weekly sessions are organized in four phases: Getting Started (sessions 1 to 3), Core Revisiting Sequence (sessions 4 to 9), Midcourse

Review (session 10), and Closing Sequence (session 11 to 16). Each phase contains some version of multiple core components. The Getting Started phase includes assessing current symptoms and impairment and taking the patient's history. The treatment is described, and the patient's active participation is enlisted. Personal goals are identified, and a conjoint session with a close family member or friend is held. While this phase contains most of the material in the first component, background information may be reintroduced in a later session if the therapist decides there is a need for review.

The Core Revisiting Sequence (sessions 4 to 9) includes most of the imaginal revisiting procedure; introduction of situational revisiting of places, people, and activities that have been avoided since the death; and beginning work with memories and pictures. During this phase the therapist also attends to work on positive emotions and aspirational goals. The Midcourse Review is used to summarize progress to date and decide on the main focus for the closing sequence. Work on role transition and/or an interpersonal dispute may be pursued in this last phase as needed. Termination is also addressed in the closing sequence. Beginning with session 10, the patient is reminded at each visit about the number of sessions remaining. The termination discussion includes continued review of progress and plans for continued progress after the treatment is over. Feelings about ending the treatment are also discussed.

CGT sessions are structured throughout the treatment to work on the loss early in the session and work on issues related to ongoing life later in the session. This sequence is important. The rationale is based on two principles of effective processing of highly distressing affects. One is that processing intense dysphoric emotions is facilitated by the ability to access the emotional state and also to set it aside. The second is that positive emotions can help mitigate the stressful consequences of negative affect.

SUMMARY

Complicated grief as we understand it can be reliably identified using a simple screening and evaluation procedure. The syndrome has been identified throughout the world and is associated with a range of negative consequences and impairments. Our clinical research team has developed a simple, short-term intervention that can be reliably administered and is associated with significantly better treatment outcomes than both antidepressant medication and psychotherapy that is proven effective for depression. This chapter reviews the basic principles and procedures that can be used to assess and treat bereaved people suffering in this way.

There is some confusion about what it means to experience complicated grief and perhaps the field should debate this. However, while debates are often entertaining, our clients may benefit more if each of us brings to the consulting room as much knowledge and clear thinking as we can muster. We have taken an approach that rests on careful definition and testing of concepts and procedures. We have done painstaking work to describe our procedures and to design and carry out rigorous clinical research to test their efficacy. We train therapists in these methods. This does not mean we think our approach is the only way to help people with complicated grief. However, we do hope that professionals who encounter these individuals will be familiar with our methods and consider when and how they might use them.

M. Katherine Shear, MD, is the Marion E. Kenworthy Professor of Psychiatry and Director of the Center for Complicated Grief at Columbia School of Social Work. Dr. Shear has spent decades conducting clinical research in anxiety, depression, and related disorders. She developed complicated grief treatment and confirmed its efficacy in three large National Institute of Mental Health-funded studies. She is widely recognized for her work in bereavement, including both research and clinical awards from the Association for Death Education and Counseling and invited authorship of articles for UpToDate *and the* New England Journal of Medicine.

REFERENCES

American Psychiatric Association. (2013). Diagnostic and statistical manual of mental disorders (5th ed.). Washington, DC: American Psychiatric Association.

Bui, E., Mauro, C., Robinaugh, D. J., Skritskaya, N. A., Wang, Y., Gribbin, C., ... Zisook, S. (2015). The structured clinical interview for complicated grief: Reliability, validity, and exploratory factor analysis. *Depression and anxiety, 32*(7), 485-492.

Cozza, S. J., Fisher, J. E., Mauro, C., Zhou, J., Ortiz, C. D., Skritskaya, N., … Shear, M. K. (2016). Performance of DSM-5 Persistent Complex Bereavement Disorder Criteria in a Community Sample of Bereaved Military Family Members. *American Journal of Psychiatry*, *173*(9), 919–929.

Maciejewski, P. K., Maercker, A., Boelen, P. A., & Prigerson, H. G. (2016). "Prolonged grief disorder" and "persistent complex bereavement disorder", but not "complicated grief", are one and the same diagnostic entity: An analysis of data from the Yale Bereavement Study. *World Psychiatry*, *15*(3), 266–275.

Mauro, C., Shear, M. K., Reynolds, C. F., Simon, N. M., Zisook, S., Skritskaya, N., … Glickman, K. (2016). Performance characteristics and clinical utility of diagnostic criteria proposals in bereaved treatment-seeking patients. *Psychological Medicine*, 1–8.

Miller, W. R., & Rollnick, S. (1991). *Motivational interviewing: Preparing people to change addictive behavior*. New York, NY: Guilford Press.

Prigerson, H. G., Maciejewski, P. K., Reynolds, C. F., Bierhals, A. J., Newsom, J. T., Fasiczka, A., … Miller, M. (1995). Inventory of complicated grief: A scale to measure maladaptive symptoms of loss. *Psychiatry Research*, *59*(1–2), 65–79.

Shear, K., Frank, E., Houck, P. R., & Reynolds, C. F. (2005). Treatment of Complicated Grief: A Randomized Controlled Trial. *JAMA*, *293*(21), 2601.

Shear, M. K., Reynolds, C. F., Simon, N. M., Zisook, S., Wang, Y., Mauro, C., … Skritskaya, N. (2016). Optimizing Treatment of Complicated Grief: A Randomized Clinical Trial. *JAMA Psychiatry*, *73*(7), 685.

Shear, M. K., Simon, N., Wall, M., Zisook, S., Neimeyer, R., Duan, N., … Keshaviah, A. (2011). Complicated grief and related bereavement issues for DSM-5. *Depression and Anxiety*, *28*(2), 103–117.

Shear, M. K., Wang, Y., Skritskaya, N., Duan, N., Mauro, C., & Ghesquiere, A. (2014). Treatment of Complicated Grief in Elderly Persons: A Randomized Clinical Trial. *JAMA Psychiatry*, *71*(11), 1287.

Index

A

American Psychiatric Association (APA), 1, 5, 19, 57, 97, 100

Antidepressants, 8, 24, 57, 62, 74, 120, 147

Anxiety, 19, 24, 34, 35, 81, 144

Association for Death Education and Counseling, 8, 14, 57, 66, 86

B

Bereavement exclusion, 8, 9, 11, 19, 57, 62

Bramley Rabbit Story Series, 106

C

Center for Complicated Grief, 135, 147

Childhood traumatic grief, 12, 13, 95, 98, 99, 100

Complicated grief

    Assessment of, 2, 31, 45, 62, 80, 81, 83, 96, 97, 116, 134, 142

    Definition of, 2, 6, 7, 13, 19, 43, 44, 46, 47, 48, 50, 60, 62, 97, 115, 132

    Disorder, 1, 11, 12, 31, 33, 56, 57, 58, 61, 100

    Reactions, 78, 99, 100

    Risk factors, 26, 71, 73, 75, 82, 83, 84, 85, 96, 133

    Symptoms, 11, 47, 79, 95, 111, 114, 127, 135

Complicated Grief Treatment (CGT), 127, 136, 137, 145

Conditions for Future Study, 12, 19, 32, 58, 100

D

Depression, 1, 8, 9, 10, 12, 13, 14, 17, 19, 24, 26, 35, 39, 56, 57, 61, 81, 84, 99, 147

Diagnostic and Statistical Manual of Mental Disorders (DSM), 1, 5, 19, 32, 57, 97, 134

Disorder

    Mental, 5, 12, 14, 32, 56, 57, 59, 60, 62, 65, 138

    Major Depressive, 1, 6, 8, 9, 10, 12, 39, 57, 62, 120

    Panic, 120

    Pathological grief, 11, 12, 31, 56

    Persistent complex bereavement (PCBD), 11, 12, 19, 31, 32, 44, 58, 60, 100, 124, 134

    Posttraumatic stress, 11, 24, 31, 96, 115

    Prolonged grief, 1, 11, 12, 33, 44, 75, 99, 100, 135

    Separation anxiety, 11, 12, 13

Dual Process Model, 20, 115

G

Grief

    Abnormal, 55

    Absent, 6, 18, 25, 51

    Acute, 8, 64, 127, 130, 131, 133, 139, 142

    Adaptive, 82

    Anticipatory, 78, 79, 82

    Chronic, 1, 7, 13, 18, 20, 22

    Delayed, 2, 7, 13, 18, 22, 23, 32, 43

    Disabling, 2, 31, 32, 33, 38, 40

    Disenfranchised, 7, 97, 98

    Exaggerated, 2, 7, 18, 23, 24

Don't Miss Out
on our accompanying program!

Our fantastic Living with Grief® program includes two hours of engaging education. Makes for an excellent supporting resource for your *When Grief is Complicated* book.

Includes:

- In-depth discussion with expert panel members Kenneth J. Doka, PhD, MDiv, Robert A. Neimeyer, PhD, and Therese A. Rando, PhD, BCETS, BCBT
- Moderated by Emmy-award winner Frank Sesno
- First-person accounts of complicated experiences with grief
- Interviews with additional experts

Available in webcast and DVD format!

Popular books
available *now* from
Hospice Foundation of America

Titles include:

Managing Conflict, Finding Meaning: Supporting Families at Life's End

The Longest Loss: Alzheimer's Disease and Dementia

Living With Grief: Helping Adolescents Cope with Loss

Improving Care for Veterans Facing Illness and Death

End-of-Life Ethics: A Case Study Approach

Beyond Kübler-Ross: New Perspectives on Death, Dying and Grief

Journeys With Grief, A Collection of Articles about Love, Life and Loss

HOSPICE FOUNDATION
OF AMERICA

www.hospicefoundation.org

(202) 457-5811 phone
(202) 457-5815 fax

The mission of Hospice Foundation of America is to provide leadership in the development and application of hospice and its philosophy of care with the goal of enhancing the U.S. health care system and the role of hospice within it.

NOTES

NOTES